THE MOTORCYCLE PRESCRIPTION

Scrape Your Therapy

Michael Stewart

Beaten Stick Press

ISBN-978-1-7387543-4-2 ebook
ISBN-978-1-7387543-5-9 paperback
ISBN-978-1-7387543-6-6 hardcover

For Barb, riding together.

CONTENTS

FORWARD

How many times have you heard the self-help wellness mantra, 'be the best you can be?' Perhaps you became curious, purchased one of the thousands of programs, and enthusiastically dove in, only to be left thinking, 'Is this it? Really, this is my best self. What's wrong with me?'

Welcome to the club of those who require something beyond deep breathing followed by a gluten-free snack to achieve nirvana. What if we replace the secret ingredient in these traditional programs with something unconventional—how about 'motorcycles?' Let's see if it works.

> **Motorcycles** saved my life, and they can do the same for you. If you have been struggling or even if you just want to make an improvement in your life, **motorcycles** could be the answer. Through **motorcycling**, happiness and clarity are absolutely achievable. They may seem far away, but **ride** with the concepts provided, and you can find a new path, one full of positivity and excitement. Nothing is out of reach when you believe in the **power of motorcycles to do good**.

> Now is the time for you to **climb on** and follow the **endless highway** to find everything in life you desire. I hope you go out and buy a **motorcycle** and never let go.

I call it the Motorcycle Prescription.

Scrape Your Therapy!

INTRODUCTION

A single tire track marks the beginning of a lifelong journey. The process of learning to ride begins in driveways, bumping along dirt trails, circling cones in parking lots, rattling across fields, and speeding down back roads. Those who graduate become licensed SQUIBs—those squirrely riders with underdeveloped skills prone to mishaps like paint scuffs, road rash, and bouts of terror. Yet, amidst this turbulence, a profound shift occurs—a situational awareness regulator kicks in. Skills improve, bonds form, and the road's fraternity extends a silent welcome to its new members.

Ride on SQUIBS!

Hone your skills.

Scrape your pegs well and true.

For some, like my young cousin Lenny, progression stalls at 'Born To Be Wild Blockhead.' Their motorcycle prescriptions require tweaking. Fueled by an overabundance of youthful bravado and narcissism, SQUIB Blockheads are locked in a dangerous struggle. Even I, seasoned as I am, have Blockhead Moments. Regression is part of the journey.

Some folks kick motorbike tires, only to find they have a reptilian-like need to slither across the planet sealed inside cages. The art of balance on two wheels, or three, is not for everyone.

Sadly, for a few unfortunate souls, motorcycle passion comes at a steep price. Recently, my friend Big Guns was slingshoted too soon to his celestial ride. The Motorcycle Prescription requires participants go all in.

Those who persist come to grasp the MAGIC in the machines and the JOY found on the endless highway or dirt trail. My Guzzi riding friend Marta talks about the need for skilled bikers to fine tune their Motorcycle State of Mind to reach what she dubs 'top-tier,' a level beyond 'skilled rider.' It's the equivalent of what traditional mindfulness folks call 'nirvana' or 'bliss.' According to Marta, I'm a couple of adjustments away from being top-tier.

Is that so, Marta, I think? *Who appointed you the oracle of motorcycle enlightenment?* It doesn't matter because everyone's entitled to their opinion. Both Marta and I have quite a few.

When Marta questions my permanence in the upper echelons of ridership, I answer, "nonsense," but honestly, I suspect she's on to something. If permanent top-tier is the equivalent of reaching what spiritualists call the state of perfect happiness, that's a big ask of someone who practices Curmudgeonly Jackassism. But if the solution is simply to ride more, why not go for the brass ring?

There are tons of self-help strategies available. Toss the word 'wind therapy' in the mix and perplexed NimRods (folks unable to grasp the attraction of two-wheels), roll their eyes and scoff. Traditional practitioners can't wrap their enlightened heads around the fact that some of us require stronger medicine.

The power of motorcycles to do good is an intangible force attached to a machine that's far removed from calm and inward facing. My friends explain the power this way: "The wheels are round and they roll," meaning 'either you get it or you can shove an incense stick up your ass.' They haven't won many traditionalists over.

To reach the zenith of riding, 'top-tier,' requires that skilled riders work on their mental agility. The process is comparable to a musician moving beyond proficient to virtuoso. Both music and riding provide stimulation along with lifelong educational opportunities. Experts agree brain exercise is vital for mental health. However, there is an immense chasm between playing a musical instrument and riding a motorcycle. A sloppy musician may draw jeers and be booed off stage, but riders with lazy skills can be maimed or slaughtered. If you're a musician, don't sweat hitting a sour note. If you drift wide on a motorcycle, you may become a hood ornament.

Many folks attempting to be 'the best they can be' stall out along the way. The solution doesn't strike a chord and so they give their self-improvement attempt the heave-ho, perhaps turning to a simpler practice like mini-golf, street drugs, munching cheese puffs, or building bird houses.

Don't do that!

Stick it out.

Scrape your pegs.

◆ ◆ ◆

Scrape Your Lists, The Motorcycle Files

Reader, before going further, please read the fine print. As you proceed, you may become puzzled by some of the odd capitalized words used in *The Motorcycle Prescription*. Words like 'NimRod' or terms like 'Motorcycle Narcissism.' If they make your head ping, check out *Scrape Your Lists, The Motorcycle Files*. The book includes definitions of the vocabulary my friends and I use to share our riding experiences. *Scrape Your Lists* is the motorcycle experience described in point form.

The words are used throughout the *Scraping Pegs* book series.

PART ONE: PRERIDE

CHAPTER 1 – LETTING GO

I consider myself a lucky man. Can you imagine being an avid poetry fan and out-of-the-blue William Wordsworth moves in across the hall? No? How about hearing horrible engine noises and discovering nothing more than the turn of a wrench was required?

I'm fortunate because many years ago I found my elixir on the Road to Joy. Above me, only sky. Birds saluting. Nature whistling. Freedom ringing. My machine humming, 'yippee-ki-yay, yippee-ki-yo.'

You've been there, right? Experienced those moments when life seems to unfold its blessings at every turn. "Congratulations," it beams like a proud parent. "You've nailed it, my child."

To be fair, my time spent on-motorcycle hasn't always been a fairytale. I've logged plenty of shitty miles. No different from our hypothetical fan when Willie Wordsworth declared, "I'm switching from poetry to the lucrative superhero fantasy genre." Life happens and like overfilled oil, the truth always seeps out. When it pisses me off, I ride to shake it loose.

Not only do physical conditions like the weather and Road Vomit traffic put the skids on wind therapy, without the right mindset, moving beyond 'skilled rider' is a dead end. All therapies have a mental barrier. For example, visualizers often get stuck in a mindset where they are unable to move beyond erotic fantasies.

"The secret," Mr. Martin Holmes, aka 'Smarty Marty' advises, "lies in mastering the art of letting go." When Smarty's at home in San Jose, California, he volunteers with a therapeutic riding group. Recently, he visited my friend Marta. They're old college buddies. "Let's have a go at pushing you to permanent top-tier, Mike," he offered.

Whatever, Smarty. I had no doubt about who stuck that gem in his mind.

Speaking of letting go, I did, a few years ago. Adhering to the laws of physics, I rocketed into a stretch of asphalt like a haywire North Korea missile.

Smarty Marty doesn't talk about the Motorcycle Lottery, preferring to stick to motorcycling's high road. He focuses on 'The POWER,' the power of motorcycles to do good. "In our therapy groups, we seek to guide participants to a state of lightness, shedding the heavy burden of inner turmoil." What he means is those irritations fueled by love, hate, jealousy, revenge, shame... any of the human conditions we all experience that are a pain in the ass. "For some, riding is the perfect catalyst to release anxiety... to learn to let go."

I get it. The 'POWER' is like a religion with hard edges. One can study all the holy books ever written. Endlessly watch top-rated TV preachers. Donate pews full of money to social causes, but only those with true faith find the keys to heaven. Many people ride but never really let go, just as most church goers fail to sense God's presence.

When I met Smarty, I figured he'd launch into one of those self-help spiels. *Buy my special sauce! Step this way to be the best you can be. I know the way.* That sort of thing.

Marta may have warned her friend to go easy. 'Mike's a hard sell. A bit of a curmudgeon.' She doesn't understand the art of not giving a shit.

For years, my approach has been simple: Ride and let the wind blow my mental clutter away. If it failed to work, ride faster. Take an off-motorcycle break and repeat as necessary.

'Good enough,' I'd congratulate myself as I pushed the kickstand down. Marta's point is that I haven't taken full advantage of wind therapy. "It's time to step up to top-tier, Mike. Or you'll fade out." I have a history of being inconsistent. Like whining about being bored. Or complaining about my sore ass. Or being an adrenaline junkie.

I'm not one to meddle, which makes me suspicious of crusaders like Smarty Marty. As I said, I'm a natural curmudgeon; it's darn near impossible to rewire skeptics like me. I'm the 'just give yourself a kick in the ass,' or 'bury your head in the sand' type. Although I will admit, I was moved by the handmade card I received from an underprivileged kid, expressing gratitude for my generous donation to Big Guns' Teddy Bear Run years ago. Undoubtably, it was a forced thank-you, still it touched me. At least until my friend Conrad spotted it and said, "The motorcycle looks like it has a snake's head." Do you see why I need to ride?

Despite my stoic front, Smarty Marty wasn't deterred. He suggested I could assist from behind the scenes, offering a road warrior's perspective on The POWER's therapy and motivational materials. I'd be helping people get through traumatic events. Soldiers with PTSD. People in crisis and any rider wanting to up their game.

Marta added: "At the same time, The POWER will rub off on you, moving you up to top-tier."

Really, Marta? I was beginning to feel picked on. I'm not as thick skinned as I appear to be.

"Are you on board?"

I answered with a noncommittal shrug. I'm not the type to join the Rosicrucians, Scientologists, Red Cross, Feed The World, or any other crusading movement. My helmet overflows with my own trash.

"Do it for yourself... to improve your future rides," Marta said, urging me to consider the benefits.

In an unexpected twist, Smarty tossed the idea of motorcycle camping into the mix. "I have a feeling camping can extend the experience... nudge the process higher. Picture this: a crackling campfire, the whisper of leaves, the distant howl of a coyote, and your motorcycle waiting."

That pushed me over my high oil mark, prompting a firm response. "Camping is a solid, N O. No!"

I'd planned a solitary ride, unencumbered by gear, to visit my brother, disposing of my accumulated trash along the way. Now The POWER threatened to screw that up .

"Be good to see Ron," I remarked to my wife, Dori, when I revealed my road trip plan. Having family members scattered around is a motorcyclist's godsend, providing solid justifications to 'get the hell out of Dodge.' "Been too long," I added after she shot me her signature penetrating stare—the kind that wordlessly seemed to ask, 'What about the chores at home?'

Visiting family isn't just a noble act; it's the perfect rationale. Saying 'I need to ride to clear my head' can spark heated debates about priorities and wellness. 'Which is more important, me or playing with your toy?'

"How long's it been? Two or three years since I've seen my brother?" Playing my ace, I spread my hands wide, emphasizing the undeniable importance of family ties. "Family's a little more important than chores, right? I'll paint the trim when I'm back."

CHAPTER 2 - SOUR CREAM

As I pressed my key into the slot, Cam's thunderous command reverberated off the concrete floor. "Participate or die!" Armed with the capability to fire up the engine, play a few low notes, and drown him out, I chose to ignore the outburst. Again Cam raised his voice: "Participate or die!"

Really, Cam? Though I admired his fervor, riding shouldn't be a call to battle stations. Passion has its limits, and death is unavoidable. *Participants die too, Cameron.* I'm a motorcycle zealot, but my world isn't confined to two wheels. After all, I wasn't born riding. To remain grounded, I've dabbled with a range of activities, from mindful meditation and journaling to more extreme measures, like drinking heavily and primal screaming, all with disappointing results. Should I try fire-walking? Competitive hot dog eating? Qi Jong? Micro-dosing? Whirling Dervish dance? Do you see why I'm grateful motorcycles found me? Taking my motorcycle prescription is pretty simple.

Despite what Marta says, riding almost always cleans my palate of that bitter real-world aftertaste.

Cam should come up with an honest call to action. How about, 'Bikes are made to ride, so let's hit the road?' Something sensible, but not lame, like my example. The dilemma is this: words can't convey the MAGIC in the machines.

Dori doesn't holler 'participate or die' or anything else when she slides into her little EV. Crawling over the earth inside a cage isn't therapeutic. Sure, automobiles have their place—carousing in your youth and hauling hardware supplies later in life. Recreational riding transcends locomotion; it's a celebration.

A tap on the shoulder interrupted my train of thought. Key out, visor up—I turned and saw Cam waving as he exited my garage.

"Sorry." It was my wife, Dori, speaking. "I need sour cream." Her expression silently commanded, 'Could you please? Be a dear.'

Her request lingered like a wisp of exhaust smoke, her eyes issuing a silent call to action. Cam's militant mantra ricocheted across my mind as I considered asking, 'why not use milk? Who really needs sour cream?'

But then, Dori's stern gaze, formidable as an approaching storm front, brought me back to reality. She used her 'I mean business' glare: if I don't get sour cream soon, there will be trouble! Her threat was the distant rumble of thunder when you're on the road and miles out from the Shit Creek Motel.

One of the things riding taught me is: life's too short to be entangled in Sour Cream Wars. Dori needed to fulfill a commitment—bring healthy muffins to yoga class. On the other hand, I was 'playing with my toy.'

"Would you mind popping by the store? Be a dear. Take your bike. It'll make a nice ride for you. Oh, and I told Cameron you're busy."

Gee thanks. Dori doesn't find the intricate dance of balance fascinating. The MAGIC in the machines eludes her; she cannot fathom the difference between going to the store and riding with a friend.

Back in the day when we rode two-up, Dori never appreciated

the wind's whispers. "What's wrong with your windshield?" she'd ask. "Can't you get a bigger one?" The act of bringing muffins to yoga class is what makes Dori happy. I suppose we each find joy in our own way.

Marta quotes Robert Sherwood to explain the phenomenon. "We each come from our unique backgrounds and experiences. That's what makes each of us different and life interesting."

Speaking of being different, Dr. Peggy, whom I call 'Pissy' behind her back, takes the cake. I'm convinced Pissy was booted off her planet. She's not a real medical doctor and is needlessly taking up space on Earth. "Motorcycles are unnecessary and harmful," Pissy repeatedly warns, her disdain as obvious as a blowout. A good part of her venomous hatred can be pinned on her neighbor Pete Hagen's loud pipes and early morning departures.

After my accident, I tagged along with Dori and Pissy to mindful meditation classes but failed miserably. Dr. Peggy blamed it on, "motorcycles… they scrambled your brain."

Return to your planet, Pissy.

I'm like the UN. I tolerate Dr. Peggy in order to prevent hostilities—a sour cream nuclear meltdown. But boy, do our interactions pile up my mental trash. It's another reason I'm making a road trip to visit my brother Ron.

The grease-stained tools in my garage have long been a testament to my DIY history of triumphs and haphazard mishaps. The smell of the room always comforts me, a unique blend of motor oil, cleaning products, a faint trace of rodent droppings, and fresh air. It's my domain. I kicked a rubber mallet to the side and pulled my helmet on, thinking, upstairs is so different. The impending aroma of baking promised to transform it even more. I rolled forward, preparing to fetch sour cream at Country Grocer.

I'm sure Dori figured I would have a blast 'playing with my toy.' But it doesn't work like that: wind therapy requires... well, wind. Preferably on the Road to Joy, not conducting a strip mall sour cream mission.

As I drove, the wind gently caressed me, but it was not enough—I failed to merge with my surroundings. Wind therapy and meditation are similar in that both therapies work best when practiced under optimal conditions. City life, with its traffic lights and other constraints, is a cage. The expansive world had dwindled to a mere seven blocks around Country Grocer where, instead of boundless possibilities, only sour cream awaited.

I put away my gloves, helmet, and jacket, morphed into a shopper, and made my way to the dairy section at the back of the store. Sour cream comes in three sizes. To be safe, I grabbed a large container of regular and light. As I passed bulk foods I thought, I'm here, may as well check out what's on sale. So, I purchased a small bag of soft black licorice and another of the unsalted mixed nuts.

Back in the parking lot, nibbling my snacks, the soft texture of the licorice blended with the crunchiness of the nuts to ignite a firestorm of flavors. As I rested one hand on my handlebar, each chew liberated my senses, like navigating a series of curves, free from the shackles of civilization, surrounded by surprises, making love to the road, and bulking up on Motorcycle Gratitude. Is it possible the licorice - nut combo acted as what meditators call an "anchor" or "point of focus," returning my mind to pleasant thoughts? But before long, my bliss was interrupted. Irritating bits of black goo were welded to my teeth.

I picked at my teeth and spat, a reminder that not every ride is smooth sailing. Life is like that. At times we hit long stretches of sticky black licorice or slippery patches of sour cream.

On the way home, a dude waved, acknowledging the unspoken bond formed by our shared passion and the sense of unity within our community. My subdued response conveyed, 'just on a sour cream run, buddy.' Young Rider was likely meeting the boys to go for a rip.

Watching the inexperienced rider veer left, crossing the center line, I pondered, do city intersections possess their own unique rhythm? The trifecta, the Holy Trinity of approach, apex, and exit? A tire may slip. The bike may drift. Fear can grip with an unforgiving hint of doom.

Junior rider's audacious maneuver caught my attention as he raised the front wheel and tore down the street. 'Participate or die,' his bike seemed to scream! He had yet to learn that reckless youthful exuberance is a barrier to reaching top-tier. Conrad's often-repeated sentiment came to mind. "Young riders are fuck'in stupid."

While mulling over Conrad's proclamation and Martin's, "young riders have a long way to go to master the art of letting go," the engine's hum became a calming backdrop to my thoughts. Then, with a shout of "participate or die," in my mind, I twisted the throttle and imagined leaning sharply into the next turn, before tearing past the Healy place. In reality, I proceeded gently, not wanting to upset my sour cream cargo.

Cars lay at rest along our block, resembling dozing sloths, while beneath me, a dormant brute force awaited my command. I balanced on a two-wheel tightrope between danger and JOY. Sour cream was my governor, keeping me slow and steady.

I hold this belief to be true: the best muffins are under-baked. In my mind, it's an indisputable fact. Why is it even up for discussion? Let's agree and move on. It's not like we're debating 'which is the best brand of motorcycle oil.'

But no. Dori is a zealot when it comes to recipes. What is it with bakers? They're as unyielding as traffic cops or bikers wed to a specific brand. Smarty Marty says rigidity is our enemy because it can hinder being present, which is a big part of The POWER. The fact that I'm flexible about bake times and can appreciate under-bakes demonstrates I've got the right stuff to be top-tier.

After years of debate, I wore Dori down and was granted an under-baked exemption. "Extract two or three only!"

"Fine." I'm not an unreasonable man. "Observe the texture," I advise when I check her baking. "The consistency should be that of firm pudding, not cake."

"Eat at your own risk."

Devouring a couple of under-baked muffins, with their gooey texture, is a small, delicious act of defiance. I enjoy giving the baking establishment the biker salute.

Am I being disrespectful? "A great deal of expertise goes into determining bake time and temperature," Dori says.

"Kids are born with minds uncluttered by conventions. And they love raw dough."

"Then they stop pooping in their pants, evolve and gain mature tastebuds."

Technically, I enjoy my muffins medium-rare, not as raw dough. Although when Dori isn't looking, the kid in me dips a finger in the mixing bowl.

I carried the muffins when, as part of my post-accident therapy plan, I attended group with Dori and Pissy. The sessions were held in a church meeting room, which was intimidating with the Big Guy looking on. Striving to blend in, not standout as someone who flouts societal norms like baking times and certain road signs, I chose not to wear my tee shirt that says: **I Don't Give a Shit** or the politer version: **Tell Someone Who Cares**. Our leader was an expert, so I remained earnest and sat erect. When instructed to do so, I focused on my breath without making smart-aleck remarks. Dr. Peggy nodded. 'The jackass is improving,' she must have thought. But I could not stop my mind from drifting to memories of road trips. Plus, I had an urge to slit the throat of a group member repeatedly clearing their throat. I wasn't supposed to be glancing around, but when I did, I wondered, what's wrong with me? The others looked so sincere, each radiating a spiritual glow. Desperate to belong, I closed my eyes and bobbed, mimicking my classmates.

The leader clapped, sparking a discussion about conscious awareness. She asked if we could recall our original mind before our first thought. I went all-in, trying to clear my brain of all thoughts, but was unable to block Conrad's words: "I went to mindfulness class once. It was so fuck'in stupid."

Was Dr. Peggy right? Had motorcycles killed off my ability to be at one with the world simply by sitting cross-legged on the floor?

The instructor, sensing my frustration, suggested, "Try adding aroma therapy scents or a mantra to improve your focus, Mike."

How about I add new tires, a custom seat, or one of those blinking brake lights instead, lady?

Afterward, Kenny and Pety served pound cake that was over-baked, dry and bland. I was proud to be associated with Dori's muffins, which were far superior.

◆ ◆ ◆

I went into mindfulness therapies, imagining I'd hit a grand slam home run of inner peace, unleashing a new improved version of me. But my reality was different—I never got on base. I was out of place, like a bagger at a hill climb or an under-baked muffin amongst recipe purists.

After my second session, Dr. Peggy advised, her voice saturated with a tone of self-help authority, "Your motorbikes are a crutch, Michael... they're like shackles holding you back.

You need to liberate yourself, both physically and emotionally. Don't let them enslave you. It's time to break free."

"We could sell your bike," Dori suggested, her eyes gleaming. "Out with the noise. In with fresh beginnings... maybe new curtains, or a European river cruise."

Their words resonated in my mind hauntingly clear. I envisioned a life of serene simplicity, where the biggest worries were selecting a paint color, perfecting baking times, and remembering my mantra. Traditional mindfulness is super convenient. You don't have to service it, clean it, or spend money on it. You can disconnect when lying on park grass or while sitting in the dentist's chair before a root canal. There's no need to be constantly vigilant, worrying about situational awareness, GPS recalculations, and tire pressures. Disconnect anytime, anywhere. The simplicity of the traditional approach is appealing. Yet, the picture of surrendering my machine was that of an amputation. I'd look around at the other people in the class and wonder, what is it with you sour cream loonies?

As Dori left with her impeccably timed yoga muffins, an impulse led me to give meditation one more shot. In the quiet of my space, I sat on the floor, straight-backed, holding onto the expert's advice that "there is no right way to meditate." To extinguish my chaotic thoughts, I repeated my mantra "Moto-Skiveezs, Moto-Skiveezs, Moto-Skiveezs." Then I moved onto step two: "Create mental images of places or situations that relax you."

I thought about being on-motorcycle.

And there it was again, the irreverent chorus in my head, swearing, 'this is so fuck'in stupid.' Yet, a part of me wondered if my brain was putting up a veil, afraid I might break through and swap motorcycles for incense sticks.

"Participate or die!"

CHAPTER 3 - SMARTY MARTY ARRIVES

Bathed in the golden glow of a June Saturday morning, their helmets swinging rhythmically, five friends entered Tony's bistro. Marta arrived last, accompanied by a man sporting wind-tousled hair.

Marta, her voice tinged with pride and nostalgia, introduced the man beside her. "This is Martin Holmes, an old college friend. He's ridden up from San Jose on an R69S, a classic he restored himself."

I cringed—so much for my DIY bragging rights. Over the winter, I'd made a big deal of upgrading my monoshock.

Intrigued by the mention of Martin's R69S, our collective curiosity swelled. With a shared nod of acknowledgement, we were drawn outside to inspect a historic icon of two wheel design.

As we filed back into Tony's, Martin's firm handshakes were accompanied by "Now it starts," leaving us dumbfounded. What was starting? A quest? A confrontation? An Iron Butt Rally? He repeated, "Now it starts," to each of us in turn.

Really? Now it starts? Better watch your step, buddy!

Marta had hinted, "Marty's a bit eccentric." Being somewhat of a project bike herself, Marta's assessment had us on full alert.

"What'd you do, Martin?" Earl asked once we were seated.

"Aside from restoring bikes?"

Martin's answer was unexpected. "The up and down business."

"Elevator commissioning," Marta clarified.

"But my true passion is therapeutic riding. On motorcycles... not elevators. Harnessing the power of two wheels to do good. For veterans with PTSD and others. We also put on seminars for seasoned riders... to help them get to what Marta calls 'top tier.' It's about maximizing the journey... self-discovery... not just riding"

Marta jumped in saying, "We can all benefit," her gaze locking with mine.

The guys in the group had the same thought: sounds like a fit for SQUIB Dolores. The rest of us, Cam, Conrad, Earl, Den, Tony, and Manny, had logged many miles and were firmly in the 'Don't Tell Me How to Ride' camp. We weren't about to take unsolicited advice from a strange man in the up and down business. Marta, ever the progressive, is always open to new ideas and continuous improvement.

Sensing our skepticism, Marta challenged, "How will you know if you don't try?"

'Oh, brother,' I thought, 'another one of those crusader types.' While Martin yakked on, expanding on the nature of his advocacy, I surveyed the gang's telltale expressions.

Lordy, lordy.

Now it starts, the psychobabble.

Zen and the Art of Motorcycle Nonsense.

The man from San Francisco presents Woke Motorcycling.

Just zip your lips and ride.

Concealing a grin, I dubbed the stranger 'Smarty Marty' from the up and down world.

When it comes to fueling philosophical discussions, the men in our group are about as effective as congealed motor oil. We prefer to keep two wheels planted on or close to the ground, discussing meaningful subjects like displacement, lean angles, paint codes, and drive systems; not duality, meta-awareness, samadhi, or how to swing an incense stick.

"Some are naturally blessed," Smarty Marty said. "They ride and are fully present. It's rare. Most have rough edges that need to be smoothed out, the obscure ones... lodged in our minds."

As Smarty rambled, I had a revelation. His words, eccentric as they were, hinted at a deep wisdom. I should forget about the traditional prescription: make a pilgrimage to sit cross-legged under a Bohi tree in India and hum 'om.' Smarty Marty was suggesting: if enlightenment is what you seek, when you reach Asia, rent a Royal Enfield and tour the Himalayan valleys.

You see Dori, I'm not just playing... motorcycles can be game changers.

'So says your friend, the elevator mechanic.'

It's practical wisdom. Up or down? Takes you where you need to go. Not at all like reciting Dr. Peggy's poem 'Ode To A Daisy.'

"The secret to mindfulness is to find the method that works for you," I heard Smarty say. "If breathing and visualization only produced a sulking boredom and a sense of futility, why not try therapeutic riding?"

"You'll have to do some work; it takes more than skill and experience. Now it starts, is what I tell our community. It's intended to make folks pause and commit themselves to more than the mechanics... countersteering, braking and working the throttle. Now it starts. It's my way of saying, open your mind. It's a brand new day."

"Disconnectedness," Marta said. "Is what we call it."

Martin used the term 'motorcyclefulness.' Mindfulness achieved through motorcycling. "Riding on a deeper level. Learning the art of letting go." He took a sip of coffee before continuing. "Close to half the people we enroll end up dropping out. But for those who remain, motorcycles are game-changers. It's extremely rewarding to witness members become what we call 'explorers who have discovered.' Marty paused. "Thoughts?"

The group resembled bashful schoolboys. Marta winked and nudged SQUIB Dolores, eliciting an enthusiastic, "I think it's wonderful!"

The rest of the group stuck to familiar territory.

Manny asked, "594cc boxer twin, right? The R69S."

"Shaft drive?"

"Any trouble finding parts?"

"Didn't they boost the horsepower?"

"Some were fitted with side car lugs. Yours?"

"Original paint color?"

"Tolerates ethanol?"

When the technical questioning paused, Marty explained his choice of the R69. "It's an ideal therapy bike. Any classic connects its rider to a simpler era. Modern bikes might thrill, but they lack soul. Climb on a classic and you're part of a tradition."

It's true. Bikes produced before the age of over engineering are grounding. Ride a modern crotch rocket and your mind's on a racetrack. A chopper and you're Easy Rider. Any modern high-tech bike and you're soon bored because the machine's taken over.

"Riders take on the personality of their machines, so I loan R69 to group members to neutralize the machine effect." Martin paused, expecting one of us to interject. "Myself, I tried everything... even hypnotism. Nothing worked. I accept the value of traditional therapies... they're great if they work. But not for me. My gateway is riding."

A smile spread across SQUIB Dolores' face as she spoke. "Finding peace in riding is a fantastic feeling. I'm so glad you're sharing.

"The up and down business isn't enough. Elevators fulfill a

function, but don't change lives."

"You should spend time with Martin while he's here, Dolores," I suggested, hoping to deflect Smarty Marty's interest in taking me on as a side project to, as Marta put it, help me get over my Post Traumatic Stag Disorder.

"I'd love some tips," Dolores said.

Earl mocked, saying "Now it starts," while looking at SQUIB Dolores.

Settled then, I thought. Dolores will satisfy Smarty Marty's need for a pet project while he's on vacation. I was making good progress as it was, overcoming my trauma. Close to four years ago, my helmet skidded along Washington State Highway 20, the protective layer scrapping away, like life itself. The asphalt tattooed with my fears, the scars of an unexpected date with mortality... well, at least with the horror of becoming a lesser being. By the time the incident calmed down, it was clear MikeyBoy—the guy who rode like he was trying to qualify for the Isle of Man TT—was gone. Life had become still and unusually quiet. My love affair with motorbikes was in doubt. Beautiful legal drugs numbed my mind and injuries pinned my body down. My friends encouraged me, urging, 'Don't be a weenie. Climb back on! That's the ticket."

A year after my accident, I bought Therapy Bike. I wasn't solid, but persevered and became a different sort of rider. A 'weenie biker,' Cam proclaimed. Marta saw it differently. "Your motorcycle mindset has matured, Mike. Too bad it took going down hard." But according to Marta, top-tier was still 'over the horizon.'

Around the table at Tony's bistro, Marta turned to her old college friend. "Mike's setting off on his road trip soon," she said.

Smarty zeroed in on me, leaning closer. "We'll collaborate,

right, Mike? Integrate a therapeutic angle into your trip."

"Could be your breakthrough." Marta winked.

"Right up your alley," Earl said, playfully trying to box me in.

Tony grinned. "Mike the Giver, huh?"

"What a wonderful opportunity," SQUIB Dolores said.

"Mike would be delighted to, wouldn't you, Mike?" Marta said.

In the midst of nods and grins, the weight of expectations settled on me like a well-worn riding jacket, its history stitched into every crease. "How 'bout working with Dolores?" I reminded.

"I'm not planning a trip," Dolores answered, pointing at me. "You are."

I shot Conrad my 'get me out of trouble' look. He's good at sorting things out.

"Earles or telescopic forks?" Conrad asked, redirecting the conversation. "On your R69?"

"Built to tour," Manny chimed in.

"Technology has come a long way in the last thirty years. "Why ride an antique?" Dolores asked.

"A friend picked up an old Shovelhead," Martin began. "Fixed it up and brought it to therapy. I saw the Harley's positive impact and began my search." He paused. "Bought the R69 with Bitcoin. Digital currency and chrome, a blend of past and future".

"You actually lend out your bike?' we asked, astonished. "Are you some kind of saint?"

Smarty turned to me. "So, Mike, you're on board? You'll help? It's just a matter of reading our little blurbs. See if the messaging percolates at all. It's best done by someone at arm's length, while riding. Not much to it. What'd you say?"

How do you refuse a motorcycle saint? My reply squeaked out. "Yup."

"Terrific!" Martin raised his voice, indicating he meant what he said.

Marta beamed.

SQUIB Dolores applauded.

Conrad smirked, clearly amused by the situation.

Smarty Marty said he'd email a copy of The POWER journal. "Read it along the way. They're just ideas to spark thinking and group discussions. I'm sure you'll have ideas, Mike... for improvements."

Marta had read the journal and called it "a guide to elevating your Motorcycle State of Mind."

I was conflicted. *Who am I to be advising anyone?* I was a heretic, metaphorically prostrated in a ritual of deep reverence, yet out of place, an intruder in a sacred ceremony. Rise from the floor, prostrated charlatan! Climb on and be gone. This isn't for you. You are one of those who should refrain from volunteering. I took a sip of coffee and said, "Leaving in two days. Won't have much time to read. How about I make a donation to your therapy group instead?"

Martin finished his Tart of the Month and said, "That's one hell of a pastry, Tony." Then he looked at me. "Now it starts, Mike. And please consider camping. It could be another tool in our therapy kit."

Manny, our 'Bull of The Woods,' nodded, his gesture resonating like the solid thud of a motorcycle top box snapping shut—a sturdy affirmation amidst my uncertainties.

I looked at Conrad. *Smarty Marty thinks sleeping on dirt is therapeutic.* It put his entire strategy in doubt. Conrad shrugged.

"Of course, Mike will camp," Marta said. "We're all experienced motorcycle campers. What a great opportunity, Mike." Her wink carried the mischievous twinkle of a headlight beam shrouded in fog.

Camping with friends is tolerable for a night or two. There's a certain joy in complaining and frolicking with the brotherhood and sisterhood of overindulges, snorers, and whoop-de-doers. But I was traveling solo to visit my brother and had never tented alone.

"I'll pack a Tony's Cosmic Special and cinnamon roll, Mike," Tony said, trying to seal the deal.

Left with little choice, I said, "Double that Tony. Absolutely no cooking... if I agree to camp."

I looked at Marta. Sometimes having friends is a son-of-a-bitch.

At home that evening, I flicked open the POWER Journal on my tablet to see what I'd been roped into. I imagined I was attending one of Smarty's sessions, listening to his pre-ride spiel.

Now It Starts

You've tried numerous self-help methods, seeking contentment, if not happiness. Yet, your success has been minimal and your resilience is dwindling. 'Is this the best I can be?' you wonder. 'Am I doomed to remain in a state beyond help, trapped below my potential?' Or maybe you're simply too exhausted to care.

But wait, motorcycle riding offers an experience unlike any you've had before. Each individual's journey is unique. Yours may include two wheels, a journey that can restore balance. While some achieve tranquility through silent reflection, others—possibly including you—require the opposite. Rather than looking inward, motorcycles offer the world to you. On a motorcycle, there is no choice—you must participate.

You have finally arrived at where you are. The key is not in finding answers, but in taking action. You have delayed long enough. Don't hold out for the next miracle cure. There is no need to cross everything off your checklist. There is no gap. This is it. Engagement is essential and your motorcycle will demand it of you.

Before you climb on, tell yourself: 'now it starts.' You must prepare yourself to do more than simply drive.

A Fork In The Road

At some point, our journeys will present a divergence, a moment where we must make a crucial choice. Existence is a continuous stream of miraculous and mysterious moments, each one a decision point. This is exemplified in many aspects of life, but is extremely evident when riding a motorcycle. Riders are bombarded with choices; one unfolding into the next. We must embrace them. There is no choice. The miracle is not walking on water but choosing to undertake our journey with our eyes wide open to the possibilities. When we reach the fork in the road, let's lean into our new paths. Now it starts! We have choices. Which path to choose?

Reflecting on these words, I thought, no wonder Marta and Martin got along in college. Me, I'm a practical person. I switched to my route planner.

I'd attempted to encourage Conrad to read the journal, hoping he'd throw me some clever insights to pass on as feedback. "No way," he replied, thumping his chest confidently, 'I'm already top tier, so what's in it for me? Plus, it's likely too flakey for my taste."

I switched to email and gave Conrad another nudge. "Like Marta often says, it's not just a journey of miles, but of mind and spirit. I think you should read it, Conrad. I made it through the first two entries, no problem. It's in small manageable chunks."

His response was succinct: "tell me about it when you return."

I was on my own.

CHAPTER 4 – NOTES ON RIDING SOLO:

I n my garage, Manny, our backpacking Bull Of The Woods, proudly displayed a selection of gear he'd brought over. "To enjoy motorcycle camping, you need the right stuff," he advised, gesturing towards his collection, where each piece collapsed, folded, or nested.

"Thanks, but got everything I need." My dry bag hung awkwardly, resembling a sagging camel hump lashed to the pillion. It reminded me of the disfiguring dental braces that had once distorted my kids' smiles, an unholy abomination against their beauty. "Modern bikes aren't meant to tote freight. The bag messes with aerodynamics, adds weight, and complicates travel."

As I aired my grievances, Marta interjected with her usual wisdom. "If you chase two rabbits, you will not catch either, Mike," her words hinting at the need for focus and spending energy wisely. "Think of your bag as a passport to adventure, not a fashion statement. The most important thing in life is knowing the most important thing in life."

I sighed, realizing I'd have to grin and bear it, shoulder the load, and adapt to the situation. "It's not about looks; the bag will alter the bike's dynamics." I'd envisioned a smooth ride on a state-of-the-art mono-shock, stopping at cozy motels to relish some alone time. Now my plans were in disarray, all thanks to Marta's friend.

Above all, I felt disgusted with myself for breaking my rule. Post-accident, I'd established a clear directive: if I don't want to do it, I don't. Riding season's too short. Yet, here I was, feeling compromised and on the verge of heading into rattlesnake territory with little more than an old sleeping bag. I have a fear of snakes slithering into my tent and cozying up to me. My condition is what psychologists term a mix of ophiophobia and agoraphobia. I'm not the Grand Slam Explorer type, risking it all for extreme feats. Sure, I'd scrape my pegs a bit but mainly I wanted to ride, be comfortable, shed some mental trash, visit my brother and avoid lying on dirt like a reptile.

Marta put her hand on my dry bag. "Imagine this as a fun-loving leprechaun dancing on the fringe of what is possible. Tickling your perception. Jimmy Crack Corn and I don't care. This is something you want to do."

"Jimmy Crack Corn and I don't care,' I snapped, 'because I'm riding, not because I'm camping." In our group's version of the song, the rider, irrespective of race, is euphoric to be on a road trip (in the original verse, a black slave is ecstatic about the death of a white slave owner). "Jimmy Crack Corn and we don't care," the gang sings together before we ride away from life's horseshit. Truthfully, only Marta, Dolores, and Tony sing.

"I foresee hellish nights ahead if I bring my bag, hunted by snakes... suffering sleep deprivation."

"Boy, do you need to ride." Manny shook his head. "Just a few stops. It's not a big deal."

"Your wondrous wilderness motel awaits," Marta said. "I think Martin's on to something. Camping can be seen as an extension of the road, expanding horizons. Keeping the momentum going."

Manny held up his micro-burner. "Sure you don't want to borrow this?" To warm beans? Make coffee? So you won't starve to death in the great outdoors?"

"No cooking!" I declared. I'd rather drink a beer, open some packaged food, and sulk.

Since attending a seminar on journaling with Dori and Dr. Peggy, I've been maintaining various lists. As I was about to be a lone rider, I decided to start a new one.

<u>Note On Riding Solo</u>: If you're accustomed to buddies looking after arrangements, solo camping will be spartan.

Do you ever notice how certain moments feel like they've been injected with a shot of octane? Good friends. Great coffee. Tony's fresh breads and pastries. Together they kick off my day with an anything-is-possible jumpstart. It's about savoring life's simple pleasures. The aroma of gooey cinnamon rolls and good company with our machines waiting outside never fails to trigger a spark of JOY.

Elna, the Valentino Rossi of baking, brought me a just-out-of-the-oven, slightly under-baked roll. After cooling, I bit in and shared a contented glance with Conrad, who had gone for the Tart of the Month. He believes in 'mixing it up.' Why change when you've found paradise, I wondered?

Smarty Marty turned the conversation to my camping concerns. "Marta mentioned a problem with your gear, Mike."

I put on my what-the-hell-are-you-talking-about expression.

"I have a solution. Why not take Bitty... my R69? Back in its day, folks didn't have fancy luggage. Riders weren't encumbered by extras. Strap any old bag down and hit the road. It's perfectly natural, and the bike's a joy to ride. After all, you're doing me a favor and Bitty will put you in neutral territory. Free your mind. Rev up your experience. Riding therapy will benefit."

"Wow," Den said. "You'd actually lend your beautiful machine to a guy who totaled his?"

I was speechless.

Expanding on the offer, Martin added enthusiastically, "The bike's a hit wherever it goes. You'll have more interesting encounters."

A little dumbfounded, I replied, "I couldn't risk anything happening to it."

"Not a worry. Bitty is meant to be shared. It's why I bought a classic. And you'll be on-assignment."

I pictured myself rolling down the highway on the vintage beauty, a marvel of design and craftmanship. It's kind of like replacing *Motorcycle on Velvet* which hangs on my garage wall with the *Mona Lisa*. "Are you sure?" It seemed like a fair exchange for enduring tents, snakes, and conjuring up meaningful feedback.

"My pleasure. We're in this together, right?" Two wheels for the greater good. Like Johnny Appleseed, sowing the fruit of life.

Feeling compelled to reciprocate, I tentatively suggested, "Maybe you'd like to use my bike while I'm gone?"

"Sure, but don't worry. I won't ride it." Martin pounded the table and grinned. "Too recklessly."

Marta winked.

Bloody well, better not.

Cam said, "I'll show you some great back roads, Marty."

I shot Cam my wise guy look as I pictured myself on R69S, eating up miles. I'd been granted an extra dose of MAGIC.

In a spontaneous outburst of joy, Tony suddenly burst into song, with Dolores joining in to hit the high notes: "Jimmy Crack Corn and Mike don't care."

❖ ❖ ❖

Over dinner I updated Dori. "I'm borrowing Marta's friend's old bike for my trip to Ron's."

"Why? Your new one's busted already?"

I frowned, before answering, "No."

"Why on earth take an old bike when you paid for a brand new one?"

I'd failed to relate my rationale for under-bakes. There was zero chance I could explain the lure of riding an old motorcycle. "Classics are the Dead Sea Scrolls of motorbike culture, brimming with history. Anyway, it'll be more than just a ride. Marta's friend helps folks in the Bay area struggling with PTSD and anxiety issues. He wants me to review a few things... provide feedback... as a knowledgeable volunteer."

"But wasn't there something you needed to test? That expensive shock absorber, right? Wasn't that your reason for going, instead of painting the trim?"

"This bike's a classic, a rare opportunity. Something I can't pass up. Plus, I've agreed to camp... as a therapy experiment."

Dori laughed.

Before she could comment, I added, "For his volunteer work."

Dori respects charitable work and volunteer-ism. I sensed her skepticism softening. In her view, painting could not compete with meaningful giving. *Probably thinks of me as Gearhead Gandhi.* "Martin studies the mind-body-motorcycle connection. Motorcyclefulness, he calls it."

After a brief pause, Dori said, "Well, the house won't paint itself."

I detected a hint of reluctant approval in her tone. Like witnessing a crusader sailing off for the glory of god and country.

When I was recovering from my accident, I thought, 'I'd love to clean the gutters, if only I could.' Now chores collide with my guiding principle: only do what you want to do. Within reason, of course—I'm not egomaniacal. Work puts gas in the tank and food on the table. Painting buys riding credits. "My trip will be part giving back, part family visit. We're fortunate Martin's sharing his knowledge."

Dori brought the conversation back to practical matters. "The paint is in the garage. It needs to go on the house."

Dori, being perfectly capable, could easily handle the painting herself. I wondered why it always seemed to be the case that an inconvenient job popped up right when I was planning a road trip? Why not take up painting, Dori? Now it starts!

After dinner, when I took the garbage out, I checked the trim. Still in good condition, I noted. Last, another few years. I knew Dr. Peggy had been encouraging Dori to use color to express herself. Pissy writes poetry, 'Ode to a Daisy.' As for me, I find solace in motion, with two strips of synthetic rubber on the ground and one wheel following the other. My hand on the throttle, my body tilts the bike against gravity, guiding it as I eagerly anticipate the unexpected. Riding is a force of nature capable of showing you the world. It's nothing like driving a car to a poetry recital at the local paint store.

I could almost hear Marta suggesting, 'You can ride and also enjoy painting trim."

Whatever, Marta. Don't worry, I'll paint the god damn trim. It'll make Dori happy and then quickly fade. That's the nature of goals, Marta. It's documented in the POWER Journal. Have you read it?

"Great choice," I praised my wife. "I checked the paint cans in the garage. A bolder shade. Slightly darker than the old color." Dr. Peggy and Dori had spent days deciding. I know what it's like having added a custom color to a bike once. It was a real artistic conundrum.

"It's green, not brown like the old trim."

I gave my wife a hug. "The moment I'm back. Promise."

Dori's smile widened. She hadn't checked the forecast, which predicted rain following my return. But after that, I'd definitely be on it.

After dinner, I curled up with our cat Bunny, whose gentle purring underscored my quiet contemplation. Opening the journal, I said, "You can be pretty Zen-like, Bunny. Feel free to jump in with suggestions."

Sustaining

You may be wondering, "Isn't riding just for fun? How can it be therapeutic?" This skepticism is understandable. After all, riding a motorcycle is a finite experience—you can't do it indefinitely. The question arises: what's the point if, once you park the bike, you end up back at square one? Yet here you are—skeptical but willing. It's important to recognize that there is more to riding than seeking thrills. If you choose to continue, think of it as more than a hobby; riding can be an exercise in perseverance, shaping your resilience and perspective in profound ways.

Changing your worldview takes time and commitment. Took me years, partly because I didn't remind myself before I got on—it's about more than just covering miles. But now my motorcycle is my sanctuary, my lifeline. It's where I find balance and clarity, and this understanding has gradually shifted my perspective.

But what about the time when you're not riding? Build gratitude and it will sustain you. The positive effects of gratitude on the brain are well-documented and I've found that the moments I spend riding are among those I'm most grateful for. This gratitude doesn't just disappear when the ride ends; it remains. It's a continuous source of wellbeing, a reservoir of strength and positivity to be drawn from in everyday life. So, no, it's not necessary to ride constantly. The key is to cherish those moments on the road or trail and let them build a lasting sense of gratitude.

Your Quest

Riding is a quest, like life condensed in time. Just as the perfect ride doesn't last long, life too is fleeting. Each moment is a treasure to be cherished.

As you listen to the hum of tires on asphalt, let it be more than just a sound; let it be your guide, a reminder of the path you've chosen. Feel the wind and the rhythm of the road, each sensation a parallel to life's journey.

Now it starts! Your quest, a meditation on the road of life. Your motorcycle is your companion leading the way. Embrace each twist and turn, just as you conquer life's unexpected challenges and lean into its opportunities. You're on a quest.

"What do you think, Bunny?" Cats don't need to ride; they have an innate ability to disconnect.

Bunny stretched and nestled comfortably on my lap, looking nothing like the cat who enjoys giving neighborhood dogs the finger.

"Life's too short to always play the tough nut, isn't that so, Bunny?"

CHAPTER 5 - CLASSY

With my arms swinging determinedly, it took forty-five-minutes of brisk walking to reach Marta's condo. I urged myself on, "Stride Legs! Each step is a triumph. You're fantastic—thank you for getting the job done."

Walking, like breathing, is instinctual—a part of the standard package and something I used to reserve for dire emergencies. Now, I'm a Legs cheerleader. They're the unsung heroes of our daily lives, yet we take them for granted. But when stumbling occurs, our frustration erupts: "Stupid legs! Lazy lungs! Do your goddamn jobs!" The reaction is not dissimilar to a broken-down motorcycle.

After my accident, Left Leg was sidelined. The challenge of regaining the ability to walk taught me to appreciate every step—at least initially. Remaining a Legs fan forever is impossible. Most of us can't stride away with the speed and grace of an elite athlete like Usain Bolt. "Plodding," the mundane activity is labeled—walking gratitude is rare. Unless it's taken from you.

My gaze set on the horizon, elbows bent at right angles, and arms swinging as if reaching for my back pocket, I quickened my pace as I closed in on Marta's. "Go, Legs, go!"

A truth about motorcycles: you need legs to ride one.

Lost in my thoughts and the rhythm of my steps, I was

nudged back to the present when I spotted Smarty Marty by the underground parking entrance. I slowed to a leisurely stroll. Scrape your pegs on a stretch of curves and your friends will kid you about being MotoGP's Valentino Rossi. Speed walk and people think you're a weirdo.

Nice day for a walk, Mike," he greeted me, clad in shorts, sandals, and a tee shirt emblazoned with The POWER.

I slowed even more and nodded. "Indeed, it is."

Soon, the key to the kingdom dropped into my hand. I paused before completing the exchange. "Go on," I insisted. "Take mine... just in case. It'll be in the driveway."

I was eager to hop on the borrowed classic, but had to endure Smarty's ramblings politely, something about how well the R69 was suited to his volunteer gig. The man could have been a Jehovah's Witness or a Mormon, preaching the virtues of motorcycling, I thought as I nodded. Eventually, the sermon ended. "Take her around the block. Let me know what you think. I'm looking forward to your trip feedback... and thoughts on camping."

Whatever, Smarty. Don't count on your bolts holding before they're torqued.

Swinging my leg over the old beemer was a breeze, thanks to its accommodating seat height. As the engine came to life, a sound resonated through the complex like a lion's waking roar. My connection with the machine was immediate and visceral. The engine's thrumming power vibrated under my fingers, pulsing rhythmically through the grips. Even at idle, the boxer engine, with its characteristic opposed cylinders, produced a subtle rocking motion with each ignition spark in the combustion chambers. The metallic clunk of the oil head boxer I once owned echoed in my mind as I engaged the clutch lever and shifted into first. I rode away, keenly aware of my unique position—undoubtably the only R69S rider on the road at that moment. Rounding the last corner, I felt like an Olympian taking a victory lap.

"Well?" Martin inquired when my helmet was off, his eyes gleaming, mirroring our mutual admiration.

"Pure motorcycle. Absolutely love it."

"It's from a time when constant engagement was demanded. Today's tech-heavy bikes make riders passive. On Bitty, you're always totally in charge, Mike. It's the beauty of older machines."

"Runs like new. I won't want to return it... I can tell you that."

"It's hard to imagine now, but the end was near for this bike, not that long ago. The seller laid it out straight. High oil consumption, low compression, leaks, vibrated like a washing machine. Looked okay outside, but like our internals, worn piston rings, tired valves, and busted seals lurked unseen. Bitty needed a total rebuild."

"Bitty? That's a peculiar name." Sounded dodgy.

"The seller's passionate about vintage machines, but not keen on our banking system. Insisted on being paid in digital currency... Bitcoin. Believes a transformation is in the works," Martin smirked. "He's waiting for an impending financial system collapse. Only those on the blockchain will survive."

I nodded, feigning crypto mining experience.

"Must say, being a renegade added an edge to the transaction." A wide grin formed on Martin's face. "Help tear down the federal reserve, the seller told me. It's a libertarian dream." He paused. "Or Vegas casino capitalism."

"Fortune favors the brave, they say. Fits the biker image, I suppose. You weren't concerned about illegalities?"

"Did my homework." Marty flicked a dead bug off the front fender. "Our transaction was above board. Paperwork's under the seat."

"Bitty... I'm not sure I like the name."

"We share a bond, Bitty and I, unbreakable like the blockchain. Hence the name."

"Always been a goal of mine... to take a road trip on a classic. Thanks so much." I masked my emotion with a cough, a lump of gratitude lodged in my throat.

"A goal?" The word seemed to bother Marty. He pondered for a moment before saying, "In our groups, one of the first thing we teach our members is to distinguish between goals and happiness. It's an important concept. We don't want them beginning their journey thinking of riding as a goal that will result in happiness." He paused, and I nodded, even though the man was making no sense. "We're told, at a young age, to create goals and we believe achieving them will make us happy. Like owning a R69 or striking it rich. We're taught that achieving goals is the pathway to happiness, but it's fleeting. Once fulfilled, we return to where we started. True happiness requires a different way of thinking. So Mike, best not to think of Bitty as achieving a goal."

Whatever, Smarty. My goal was to ride off on his bike and revel in a state of blissfulness. Here's my first piece of feedback for Mr. Holmes: two-wheels have the power to transcend traditional thinking and emotional responses. Your goal-happiness theory may not apply where motorcycles are involved.

After a manly bear hug, Martin expressed a desire for a brisk walk. I recommended a route and off he went, striding like a Paralympian.

On the way home, I gave Bitty a new name: "Classy. That's what I'll call you." And just like that, before I dismounted and still wearing a huge grin, we became a couple.

Then, standing in the driveway, I eyed the trim and felt miffed. It wasn't the effort required; it was the fact the job was unnecessary, and that Pissy had been involved in its formulation. I wondered if I dare explain 'goals' to my wife. When applied to paint, Smarty Marty's theory made all sorts of sense. 'Is it really worth it, Dori? You'll soon latch onto a new goal, like replacing the backyard fence. Do you see how pointlessness it is?'

But sometimes in life it's best to suck it up and grind it out or, as Marta would say, "take pleasure in making others happy, even if it doesn't last long."

Later I read in the POWER Journal, "goals are useful and absolutely fine to create, just don't bet your happiness bank on them. We're going to find our happiness in meaningful ways."

After reading those words, I used my memo app to create feedback. "Spell it out, Martin. By 'meaningful' you mean 'on the Road to Joy.' So the goal is to ride in order to seek JOY. It's back to my point that bikes trump your goal-happiness theory."

Truthfully, I could see Smarty's point. When educating people who aren't thinking straight, concepts must be dumbed-down.

◆ ◆ ◆

With a few hours to spare, I set up a ladder and then headed into the garage to grab a paint can. My plan was to paint one corner of the house, hoping the fresh trim color would provide Dori moments of happiness and demonstrate my commitment.

While I was opening the can, Conrad dropped by on his small dual-purpose. I quickly banged the lid tight and walked over to Classy where Conrad offered this advice: "Borrowing a classic, an irreplaceable, priceless piece of history, is madness, Mike. Are you thinking straight?"

"Classy sits low and gives a real sense of speed. I won't be tempted to dial it up."

"Still, shit happens."

I figured the odds were about one in nine million, similar to the chances of lightning striking the same place twice, or of me being involved in another encounter with a stag. "I like my odds."

"They're slimmer than winning the mega lottery, yet people

win all the time."

"Never twice. This bike demands respect... probably even from wildlife, which improves my odds."

"There's that," Conrad conceded.

I was tempted to ask my friend if he'd like to join me. But I'd made a huge production about going solo, saying it was a goal of mine. "The road will be my companion. Every bend will hold the promise of a new discovery in my solitary journey." That sort of thing.

Note On Riding Solo: When faced with questions about loneliness, I reply, "How can I be lonely when I have me for company?"

Even the most solitary rider has a bit of the herd instinct. All I had to do was whisper the code to a buddy. "Got the itch? Wanna join me? Go for a ride?"

Leaving alone was going to be tough. The remnants of recent life—vivid memories of celebrations, relationships, obligations, comforts—always cling to me.

It'd take a couple of blocks to leave them in the ditch.

CHAPTER 6 - BIG GUNS

I hate it when you're all fired up and prepped to get on with something and someone makes it all about them by dying.

Coincidentally, they were discussing the topic on a radio talk show. Is there a motorcycle killing season, like rutting season, baseball season, or haying season? Kelly, the host of CFRV's morning show, posed the question. "It's that time of the year when riders dust off their motorcycles."

Really, Kelly? We're not talking baseball.

Kelly continued, "Yesterday, tragedy struck." There was a fatality. We know there will be more. It happens every year. What needs to be done to prevent these tragic deaths?"

"Fix the potholes! The first caller was pissed about the state of city streets. "It's like driving around Gaza City."

The caller has a grudge, I thought, noting the hissing quality in his voice.

After similar observations, Kelly summarized. "So, improved road maintenance will prevent biker deaths."

Caller Barry, his voice carrying the seasoned wisdom of countless miles, disagreed. "Fixing roads won't do it, Kelly. Getting your license and going to a safety class isn't enough. Riders need to learn situational awareness, how to make quick decisions, and how to give themselves space." He spoke like one of those know-it-alls.

A senior rider wanted to "outlaw crotch rockets."

"Safety is all about being seen."

"Or expecting not to be seen."

"Obey all laws."

"Don't climb on."

"Graduated licenses. Start small."

At the end of the segment, Kelly proclaimed, "There you have it."

But what did listeners really have? A chorus of voices offered solutions, yet what tangible result was achieved? All the chatter didn't help my buddy, Bob Plett, known as Big Guns, who vanished without a solid explanation. What were Guns' last words in those seconds before his life went dark? He was indisputably top-tier, a skilled rider, yet he screwed up. Or did he? Was it simply his fate?

"Bobby, what's your dream... when you grow up?"

"Motorcycle rider," Guns would answer. From a young age, he knew he was meant to ride.

"You can be anything you set your mind to as long as you don't give up. So, what'll you be, son?"

"Motorcycle rider."

Not what parents hope to hear, but Guns was a rarity; he lived his passion. No one dreams of becoming a tire installer or landing a middle-management job. Guns had a dream, and it came true. He wasn't a failure.

"So, what do you do?" strangers ask.

"Motorcycle rider," Guns would answer. It's not like saying, 'I'm a clerk' or I'm a 'firefighter' or 'I'm a programmer.' You embody your actions. Guns rode.

It's acceptable to say, "I'm a golfer." People assume you're a financial adviser or a botanist or something similar. But say, "I'm a rider," and you're labeled a badass who flaunts society's rules and norms. Guns didn't waste time worrying about what others thought.

After my accident, once the haze of mind-numbing drugs lifted, I heard the ticking of my life clock as I gazed into the dormant darkness, engulfed by the feeling of uselessness that awaits the less functional. Fortunately, I still had a bit of my 'kick yourself in the ass' resolve left.

Experiencing a life-changing event usually deepens one's appreciation of time. People either rise from the depths of their ordeal or succumb to it.

I remember Big Guns stopping by my hospital bed. Full of good cheer, he said, "You'll have lots of time to plan your next trip, Mike."

After he left, a voice asked, "So, who are you? A person who climbed back on? A motorcycle rider like Big Guns?"

Now with my head above water, I'm the hamster who stopped running around its wheel going nowhere. I formally added 'motorcycle rider' and 'explorer' to the definition of 'who am I?' And prefixed 'Zen' to 'Curmudgeonly Jackass.'

So many people arrive at the end of the road and realize life vanished while they were by-standing. As a consequence of my thump on the head, I became determined to integrate aspirations into my daily life. It's not like I started snagging Hail Marys and diving into end zones. But you get my drift. I've become more like Big Guns. My tomorrows are purposeful. My dreams are incorporated into my present life. I guess you could say my aspirations are larger than goals.

'Seize the day' is a common expression. But we often defer, waiting, hoping to win the lottery, to have the day seize us.

When Smarty Marty learned about Big Guns, he said that the man seemed to be a rarity. "One of those who can see beyond their own experiences. Life-awareness is one thing no one can give you and money can't buy," he said. "No matter how many days you have on Earth."

Big Guns was a natural. He knew who he was. Me, I had to attend the bump-on-the-head school of hard knocks.

Throughout most of my life, other priorities and the busyness of getting by consumed me. I allowed the noise to distract me from being who I was meant to be. I trudged along with my to-do lists, lost in the minutiae. To escape from the chaos of work and personal life, I'd occasionally ride away, leaving behind all the demands and relationships of what is commonly referred to as 'the shitshow.' But I never took big steps. I never followed Big Guns' tire tracks.

For as long as I can remember, folks talked to Big Guns about changing his style, 'to ensure you'll ride many more miles.' People often resist change, and Guns was no exception. He loathed being told what to do, figuring it served him no purpose. "I'm exactly where I want to be."

I suppose death for Guns was like hitting a switch. A moment of terrifying helplessness. Priorities shift when we realize the preciousness of time, a currency of which Big Guns sadly ran out of. I pondered if Guns would have exchanged motorcycles for more time and a slower pace of life?

Living in fear is not ideal, but neither is pretending to be invincible. Fear should be a fading shadow in the rearview mirror, reminding riders to be vigilant. Big Guns acknowledged his vulnerability while confidently navigating life's unpredictable and relentless challenges.

The email announcing my Motorcycle Friend's death began, "With a heavy heart." Below the note, a dash between two dates summarized Guns' life along with this: "Big Guns was a motorcycle rider."

◆ ◆ ◆

"How are you, Michael?" Elena inquired, Tony's assistant

manager.

"Good," I answered, though my mind was preoccupied with whether it was appropriate to eat during a memorial gathering. Memories of Big Guns mixed with the aroma of cinnamon rolls baking in the bistro kitchen. Business goes on at Tony's. "Under the circumstances," I added.

We're asked daily, 'How are you?'—while grabbing coffee, purchasing oil, or at work—often by those who don't really give a shit how we're doing. We're almost always, 'good.' It's a pleasantry, no one expects or wants an honest answer. 'Good' is sufficient. We leave the perception that we're a certain type of good biker. A good worker. A good customer. A good whatever. Being good at playing your role consumes your life as you keep trudging along. So, I was "good."

To be honest, the memorial had thrown a rod into my travel plans, which was aggravating. Delayed by a day. "And you?" I asked Elena.

"Good," she said, resting her hand on the chair back. "Poor Guns."

We had gathered together to remember Bobby Plett. It's what one does, so I postponed my road trip. Truth be told, Guns would have told me to hit the road.

I overheard someone comment, "Guns took one bend too many."

The response was, "It's a matter of when, not if."

"If only," folks lamented. What they meant was, if only Big Guns had made it all the way 'round, or if only he hadn't landed where he did, or if only he believed it could happen to him. Not one person said, 'if only Guns had never ridden a motorcycle.'

"You can die choking on a cracker," I reminded Elena.

People crumpled into chairs, buried their heads in hands, and passed tissues. "We'll miss you Guns."

"The son of a bitch… why wasn't he careful?"

"A lovely man."

"He'll be in our thoughts."

"One hell of a rider."

"Such a loss."

"A carefree prince."

I nodded sympathetically, hoping Guns was 'good' where ever he was.

Memories and anecdotes were shared. I recalled Guns favored Pennzoil Full Synthetic. We were Motorcycle Friends, not close, but I knew this: Big Guns, a skilled rider, never worried about going down. We all dance with uncertainty. Gun's attitude? C'est la vie. He had a single vehicle accident and was riding solo. Into the world alone and out alone.

SQUIB Dolores had never spoken to Guns, but even so was emotional and distraught. "Not fair." Like intermittent windshield wipers, she sobbed mournfully. "Why? Why? Why?"

Why? Because we all gotta go sometime. "Guns was a good person," I said to console her. "Had a great life."

"Makes me think about selling my bike," Dolores replied. "Take the loss and move on."

Death by motorcycle was causing her to question the value proposition. It's common with SQUIBs.

Smarty Marty, who had been listening, now spoke up. "Even the Saint of Calcutta had a crisis of faith, Dolores. But your friend Guns never doubted his path. What a great way to go." Smarty was referring to Mother Teresa, who, despite her image of unwavering devotion, faced an inner struggle. In letters published after her death, she expressed deep spiritual emptiness. "Repulsed——empty, no faith, no love, no zeal. Saving souls holds no attraction. Heaven means nothing—pray for me please that I keep smiling at Him despite everything. My prayer of union is not there any longer. I no longer pray." You can't blame the blessed mother of Calcutta. Life's sanctity can be grim. That is why there are motorcycles. To ride away.

"Guns rode his path and never questioned his choice. Loved

every minute," I said. "He never had a crisis of faith."

"If Mother Teresa had been able to ride," Conrad said, "she'd have fled. Left misery and the church in her dust. She desperately needed wind therapy. Religion isn't enough."

I nodded and then Den blurted out, "My God, my God, why have you forsaken me?" After a pause, he added, "Psalm 22:1, Jesus crying out from the cross."

"Also motorcycleless," Conrad pointed out.

"So don't sell your bike, Dolores," Smarty said. "Caterpillars transforming into butterflies. That's what I call members who are new to riding."

Dolores nodded while wiping a tear away

Motorcycles offer a straightforward, tangible experience, free from the need for blind faith or unshakable religious vows. We are not obligated to take part in services, sing hymns, or read ancient books with words handed down by God, or if you're Mormon, Joseph Smith. Riders instinctively take in the complete scene, looking beyond obstacles and the unseen. Mother Teresa, bogged down without an escape pod, lost sight of her spiritual horizon. She couldn't see what was beyond her religion.

I was about to explain that Big Guns always believed he'd make it around the next corner. That the bend that brought him down unfolded into another. But Dolores drifted away to join Marta. A small group was preparing to sing *The Motorcycle Song*, Guns' favorite.

"We often seek explanations, even when there are none," Martin said.

The imperative is to keep riding. Ride far beyond the foothills. Be patient. Search until you find your secret motorcycle road. Big Guns' Motorcycle Gratitude was strong; he never suffered a crisis of faith. Ask and you will receive a motorcycle, and it will open the door.

Note On Riding Solo: Arrive solo. Depart solo. It's written in the master plan.

Guns' influence reached far beyond the motorcycle community. He was the driving force behind the annual Teddy Bear Ride, a charitable event that collected toys for underprivileged children at Christmas. I took part once. The following year, I told Guns, "Way too many bikes for me."

Guns didn't understand. How can there be too many bikes?

I've skipped the run ever since, but have always made a cash donation. Early on I received a handcrafted thankyou note from an underprivileged kid. When the cards stopped arriving, I cut back on my generosity, moving some funds from 'The Teddy Bear Run' to 'farkles'.

CHAPTER 7 - ORCHESTRATION

As the first rays of sunshine filtered in, my restless 'gotta go' urge tickled me, thrilled that today would be different, not just another day of being me. I was full of anticipation, like a sprinter in the starting blocks. "Time to get the hell out of Dodge!" I exclaimed, stepping into our kitchen, which I had recently painted to 'freshen its vibe.'

Living in Victoria on Vancouver Island, I'm subservient to ferries with their schedules and shiploads of regulations. Consequently, my early morning enthusiasm soon gave way to the reality of waiting. After brewing coffee, I settled on the living room sofa and, to make the most of my pause, opened the POWER Journal. My answers weren't to be found in a book, but 45kms (28 miles) of ocean prevented me from finding them on the continent. Anyway, I had a debt payment to make.

Up Shift

With your helmet in hand, standing beside your bike, take a moment to pause and breathe. You've already checked the tires and oil, but have you checked in with yourself? Inhale deeply once more. Experience the sensation. Remember this: life is a series of perceptions that ebb and flow in your consciousness.

Now, as you climb onto your bike, commit to being alert and fully present. Questions may arise; don't feel pressured to find immediate answers. Allow any thoughts or have no thoughts. Accept each moment without judgement. Just as you shift gears on the road, be ready to shift your mental gears. This is more than a ride; it's an exercise that goes beyond situation awareness to being fully engaged with your consciousness. So don't simply go through your old routine. Up shift and then climb on.

While pondering feedback, my train of thought was pleasantly derailed by Bunny, our feline friend, demanding attention by leaping onto my lap. "How you doing, Bunny?"

Keep the pats coming and I'll be good.

Bunny epitomizes the art of Disconnectedness. Cats are famously indifferent about fitting in or worrying about yesterday's problems. Rarely is Bunny cantankerous, but when he's bratty, I shrug. Whatever, Bunny. It doesn't take long before he's good. Me, I need to feel the wind for a few miles on an open road.

Bunny stretched and then curled up.

"Want me to read another note, Bunny?"

Whatever.

With Bunny settled, I began reading the next entry.

Zest

Could riding a motorcycle or learning to ride more mindfully be your secret sauce? Can The POWER add a sparkle to your life? Lead to inner peace? Ease your worried mind? Foster acceptance? Boost your wellbeing?

Few people are able to perpetually hang on to their natural zest for life. "Yippee ki ye," we sing right out of the gate. "Bring it on, life!" But, inevitably, one day, zest boots us in the ass and we begin ordering self-help products online or attending contemplative classes in church basements.

Some of us need a physical nudge to reclaim our zest. Motorcycles are all about changing landscapes, supplying the prod needed to move beyond the past and to stop daydreaming about the future. Turn the key and feel the magic in the machine and reclaim your zest for life. Yippee ki ye ki yo!

As I patted Bunny, he began to purr; he was still good. If I dangled a string in front of him, his zest would leap out. Then, like turning a switch, he could disconnect.

"Feedback," I said to my memo app. "Martin, how about 'Now It Starts' on group t-shirts? You're right, we must start both the engine and our minds if we're to move beyond recreational riding." I'd been guilty of just climbing on, which explained Marta's claim that I wasn't fully Top Teir.

"Holy bent sprocket!" Feedback was beginning to pile up, and I hadn't even left yet.

Gently, I nudged Bunny aside and stood. He threw me a reproachful glance before settling down again. "Don't worry, I'll be back soon." Bunny didn't look worried.

Leaving my cat to his solitude, I returned to the kitchen, poured half a cup of coffee, and went to the garage to conduct a final inspection. Looking at the bike and my gear, I reflected on Marta's orchestra analogy. Getting ready for a road trip is similar to musicians tuning their instruments and assessing the building acoustics, hoping their diligence will connect with the audience when they perform. Players loosen strings, moisten reeds, and tighten drum skins. They warm up to engage their muscle memories. Each one strives for a harmonious connection with their instrument. As the lights intensify, the performers step onto the stage, ready for a distinctive experience, their minds perfectly synchronized to their task.

"I see myself as a performer," Marta says. "Guzzi is my instrument. I check everything over meticulously, making sure all is in order, anticipating our performance. I'm charged, ready for the show. If I'm not feeling it, then it's not a good day to go on stage."

I grabbed my phone and dictated, "Feedback. Impress this upon your community, Martin: There is no obligation to climb on. Consider, is today a good day to ride?" For me, not every day's a riding day.

Then I opened the journal on my phone.

Jump Start

Joining our group is meant to be more than just a hobby—it's a journey toward rejuvenation.

It's not uncommon to be stalled or to feel uneasy. Like a vehicle with a depleted battery, left with little energy and drained of purpose, sometimes we need a jump start.

We need to stop clinging to what's familiar and automatic, even if it's stressful to change. Life unfolds as a chain of emotions tied to uncontrollable events. Holding on to old routines is a common coping mechanism, it gives us a sense of control. But are these routines a safety net or a trap? How do we give ourselves a boost?

Motorcycles take us out of the familiar. There is no choice. Embrace the transformative power of what you're about to experience. Now it starts—your jump start.

My departure wouldn't resemble the grand, dramatic opening notes of a symphony. I'm no rock star nor a classical guitar virtuoso like Segovia, yet on-motorcycle I can bring the house down. I play the two-wheel boogie.

A text popped up. 'Wishing you a fantastic trip and a great time with your brother, Mike. I look forward to your ideas, your observing mind, always working in the background. Cheers, Martin.'

Instead of replying, I added another note to my log:

<u>Note On Riding Solo</u>: Solo riders don't sign up for guided tours. Don't tell us how or where to ride or what to think.

I wondered if my trip was long enough? Is there a minimum qualifying length? The Iron Butt types seem to think so. Quick excursions can invigorate, but journeys provide a true sense of adventure. Throw a leg over the saddle, set off for a distant destination, and let your life journey unfold. Knowing the ride will continue the next morning helps to keep you in-the-moment. There will be new paths to explore, unfamiliar sights to see, challenges to conquer, weather to adapt to, and Motorcycle Friends to meet.

One thing I was certain of: I don't have an iron butt. After my accident, I adopted 'Leave Late, Stop Early' as a guiding principle.

<u>Note On Riding Solo:</u> Schedule is not up for debate when you're a lone rider.

I pulled tight the strap holding my dry bag and was set to go on stage.

CHAPTER 8 - ALONE

Just after turning the key, my phone announced a call. Reluctantly, I killed the engine and deployed the kickstand. I peeled off my gloves and dug my phone out of a deep pocket. "Morning, Cam," I responded, mustering a semblance of cheerfulness. Cam and I had shared roads and stories since our junior high days. Before my accident, we were riding twins, our styles in sync. Cam claimed we rode the way motorcycles were meant to be ridden. Now, when we pull over during a ride, his taunt is predictable, "So, still with Team Weenie, hey?"

I assured him, "No, I've switched to Team Enjoy Riding More." Back on the road, I catch him off guard and fly by. "MikeyBoy lives! Go Team Enjoy Riding More, go!"

Shaking off the initial interruption, I eased into our conversation. "Go on," I urged Cam. "What's got your goat?"

"Smarty Marty's been lecturing me. Says I've got to make a shift to master the art of letting go. To put adrenaline junkie at arm's length." I could almost see my friend's eyes rolling. "Toward whatever the hell it is, the guy's preaching."

I borrowed a phrase from Marta. "How will you know if you don't try?"

"Me, join Team Weenie?"

"Team Enjoy Riding More. State of mind... remember? Top Tier?"

"You're beginning to sound like Marta. I told Smarty what I

always say. I'm where I want to be. It's easy for you to go along with this POWER crap. You've got the guy's R69."

True, I thought, nodding silently.

After a pause, Cam reflected, "Start by balancing your need for speed... read the journal. That's what Smarty told me. Of course, Marta instigated it, just like she set you up."

"I've read bits of the journal. If you skip by the PTSD and anxiety stuff, the messages apply. Here's a quote: "Fearless doesn't mean no limits," I quoted from memory. "Fearless can make you reckless, sending you into a blind corner too fast." I paused. "It's not that you can't take corners at speed... or that you should be fearful..." Words failed me. "Just read the journal, will you?"

"You know my position. Sure, I push the limits occasionally, but I stay in control, am responsible, and have a hell of a good time. No one needs to worry about me. As for you, watch for deer."

"Classics are immune."

"Don't let a slow leak turn into a flat." It's one of Cam's sayings. We talked a while longer before his usual sign-off, "Keep the rubber side down."

As I slipped my gloves on, recalling the road trips Cam and I had shared, I felt a deep sense of loneliness. It's the solo rider's paradox: the problem with solitude is that you're alone. You find freedom, but at what cost?

I cheered myself up with this personal fact: I often find groups and crowds and Cam exhausting.

Note On Riding Solo: Lone riders give themselves permission not to be exhausted.

PART 2: THE TRIP

CHAPTER 9 - THE TWO-WHEEL BOOGIE

T he boxer engine's melody, a rhythmic pulse, resonated through the metal frame. As Classy moved, a gentle breeze flirted with me, tugging at my jacket and playfully ruffling the dry bag. My spirit started swaying.

I'm no dancer, but I can do the two-wheel boogie. Look at me everyone, I'm on the road again! Motorcycle pirouettes, those symbols of freedom, sharply contrast with the plodding rhythms of daily life.

Bathed in the morning sunshine, I glided down 'Get Out of Dodge Lane.' Dori, a fleeting silhouette in the driveway, waved. 'Don't forget the trim!'

As I lowered my visor to shield my eyes, I thought about Dori's perspective. For those witnessing a departure, it must be like bidding farewell to an adventurer embarking on a daring mission: outwardly serene, yet teeming with unseen dangers. Like being dispatched to a war zone on a UN Peace Keeping Mission.

Why does he dance the two-wheel boogie, choosing the motorcycle life when we could buy an RV and join the neighbors at The Rendezvous in The Woods? There are countless simpler ways to nurture well-being: sweat it out at hot yoga, dabble in painting, practice Tai Chi, express your inner thoughts through interpretive dance, or unwind by tapping. Need a bit more excitement? Try zip lining at one of those adventure parks where they throw in a complimentary snack with your ticket.

Countless formulas are offered to achieve happiness. "Follow this path to transform your life," experts and influencers encourage. Who doesn't want to transform their life? So we sign on, and when our metamorphosis falls flat, we whine about it —we beat ourselves up or call the cure 'a load of horseshit.' Promoters point fingers: "You lacked commitment," or "Your mind wasn't receptive."

Then there's Smarty Marty, an honest volunteer. I admired his selflessness, investing his time and resources to help others experience the joy of motorcycles. He's not overly pushy and warns newcomers, "Riding may not be for you. It's fine to move on, but do so consciously. Make it your mission not to drift through life without intention, stuck on autopilot."

Fully engaged, I rolled along like a grand marshal, my classic motorbike rendering floats, marching bands, and clowns on minibikes unnecessary—a one-man parade, free of the usual clutter and fanfare. On the sidewalk, Strawberry Anjelo was walking her rat dog. I dipped my helmet. 'Hi there, it's your neighbor, Mike, Pearly's dad. Sitting on a glorious piece of history.' Strawberry does exactly the same route every day with her rat dog in tow. She's on autopilot, I thought.

Strawberry glanced my way, revealing a frown. What was she thinking? Your motorcycle racket annoys my dog! Why aren't you walking with Pearly?

Note On Riding Solo: Lone touring riders baffle onlookers. What's wrong with them, they wonder? Antisocial? Have no friends? Not even a dog? Nasty disposition? On the lam? Why would anyone undertake a journey alone?

Strawberry is one of those who are content to stay put. She'd never have switched places with me. The routine and simplicity of dog walking was enough for her.

If Pearly was smaller, I'd have promoted her to co-pilot. Dog lovers would smile. Aren't they a cute couple? The dog's so adorable. But it's baffling, doesn't the human have friends? Is he like a spinster with cats?

Or was Strawberry entangled, waiting for the perfect alignment of circumstances before embarking on her grand adventure? Pivot Strawberry! Stroll down a different block. Now it starts!

We're naturally inclined to procrastinate, conjuring up excuses for potential failures and convincing ourselves it's not worth our time or effort. There's a nasty dog living on the next block, so I won't walk there. The hill's too steep. Snakes are in the grass.

"Now it starts," I yelled aloud, but Strawberry was now well behind me. How she loves her dog. "What's wrong with walking the same route at the same time every day if it works?" Marta would ask. No one's obligated to climb Mt. Everest.

Because it bugs me, Marta. And how will Strawberry know if she doesn't try?

Predictability makes it easy to stick to routines. In our early years, humans are utterly dependent, enduring our helplessness. Time passes and we're told, 'stand on your own two feet now', 'set your course and make a go of it.' We struggle because emotional independence is a bugger to achieve. We experience discontentment and inharmonious relationships and perhaps sign up for counseling to 'get back on course.' Then years later, some discover, a rat dog and a daily walk are all that's required. It's not up to a guru to deliver happiness. A rat dog or cat or a nature walk will do. Or possibly a motorcycle?

For Strawberry, my solo rides represented an extreme form of independence. "I need an anchor," she'd say.

"Hey Strawberry," I yelled, knowing she couldn't hear me. "When I step off, I'll be part of a vast community, larger than your dog group. Say it with me, 'now it starts!'"

You know who understands independence? Bunny—cats never run in packs. Alone broadens their worldview.

When we chatted about me going as a lone rider, Smarty Marty said this: "Research shows that embracing solitude can enhance joy and contentment. Heals the soul."

"Riding alone isn't about isolation," Marta added. "You're constantly involved and in the ideal space for positive reflection. Then put your independence in your tank bag when you step off." Marta's a master at engaging with strangers. "Those who ride alone and feel lonely have work to do."

Perhaps I should adopt Strawberry's approach? She chats with every passerby her rat dog meets, then resumes her solitary stroll. Should I pull over whenever I spot a parked bike?

I wondered about outlaw biker clubs. Hell's Angels ride in packs. Do they truly experience solitude's benefits?

Note On Riding Solo: Even on group rides, motorcycling is done exclusively inside one's self.

People are more likely to approach and connect with a rider who is alone. Ever see a tourist attempt to mingle with an outlaw gang? Even when traveling two-up, strangers hesitate to intrude on the sanctity of a couple's bond. It's not the least bit intimidating to walk up to a receptive single rider. Strangers think they're doing the lonely outcast a favor.

Strawberry, know this: I ride solo, but I'm far from alone. What better place for a Zen Curmudgeonly Jackass to find like-minded people than at a motorcycle rest stop?

As Classy rode through Big Guns' neighborhood, I offered a silent salute and reminisced about our Gold River trip and the success of last year's Teddy Bear Run. Our conversations always involved motorcycle stuff. It struck me: had Guns imagined a different path for himself, what diverse topics might we have chatted about?

I made a mental feedback note: Martin, I think you should remind your members, "riding isn't a constant. Don't be exclusive. Ask, "What are my alternates? What can I do in addition to motorcycling?"

Automatically, I looked toward Heavan. *Are you up there, Guns, looking down on me?* Riding can transport its congregation to a realm of timelessness, a space where eternal life seems probable. On-motorcycle, I often think, there is more going on than can be comprehended. I guess it's like going to church for those who worship inside cages. "Rest in peace, Big Guns."

I tapped my GPS. It consulted satellites to confirm what I already knew: I was just past Gun's place. Marta and Martin opposed using modern electronics on classics, but I defended the use of my GPS as a bridge between eras. "Just because the bike's a classic doesn't mean I must be a Luddite. Back in the heyday of R69s, curvy roads were easier to find. Now, without a thrilling ride setting, good luck."

"At least keep it to a minimum," Martin cautioned, romanticizing the notion of unplanned adventures and trusting one's gut.

Whatever, Martin. Practical people understand that blending spontaneity with technology is the best approach.

Undeterred, Martin continued, "Give yourself permission to stray." The journal underscores how society rewards self-control and adherence to rules, while simultaneously teaching us to view spontaneous behavior with suspicion. "Cast off your constraints."

"One road leads home and a thousand roads lead into the wilderness," Marta added, quoting C.S. Lewis.

I pressed the OFF button on SatNav. The route to the Swartz Bay ferry terminal was engraved on my brain. Living on

Vancouver Island means most journeys begin under the strict observance of maritime laws. Admirals keelhaul spontaneous sea captains who switch to Thrilling Ride. Rebellious ferry mavericks giving seafaring laws and norms the finger are not tolerated. My trip would begin, very much buttoned down.

Here's my route.

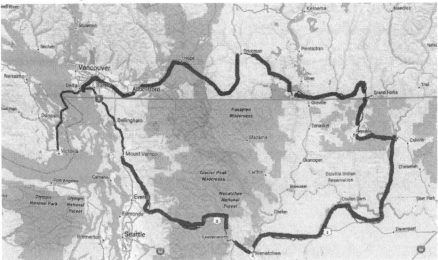

CHAPTER 10 –
BORDER CROSSING

C lassy glided to a halt at the front of a two-hundred-vehicle queue. Kids are taught, "Don't butt in!" It should be corrected to: "Don't butt in, unless you're on a motorcycle."

A truth about motorcycles: motorcycles belong at the front of the line.

Most of the bikers were alone, but we appeared to the hundreds of cagers behind us to be long-lost friends who happened to bump into one another.

A man with a friendly demeanor approached, sporting a jacket that read 'Christian Rider.' Cautious of overly enthusiastic evangelicals, I pretended to be engrossed in adjusting Classy's brake lever.

Christian's gaze was welded to the R69. I've wandered into breathtaking European cathedrals, the kind that make you exclaim, 'Holy mother Mary of Jesus,' so I understood his reverence. Caught up in the man's amazement, I revealed a bit of my Gearhead Gandhi mission. "The power of motorcycles to do good," I said, tapping Classy.

Christian's face lit up, radiating a 'no need to explain, I get it' understanding. His expression had me contemplating the profound nature of faith, how it must be like having a set of those bright driving lights that illuminate your way, attached to your brain. Faith and Motorcycle JOY together, a one-two punch, the opposite of bikers pigeonholed as sinners, bound for eternal damnation.

After I explained a bit about Martin's volunteer work, Christian stated that therapy group members must look to a higher power for solace. "We may feel we cannot be good enough for a Holy God, but God Himself provided the solution. Accept the Lord Jesus Christ as your savior. Then ride with genuine gratitude."

Really, Christian? But considering the potential downside, I've always thought it illogical not to believe. Why hold on to an 'it's all over when you die' dogma when what waits around the next bend is unknown? Suppose your number comes up in the Motorcycle Lottery and wham-o, like Big Guns, you go horizontal? Motorcycling is a risky business. Ride down the endless highway. Look at the sky and most riders understand this: there's more going on than we can comprehend.

So I nodded while mentally logging feedback. *Martin, talk to your members about spirituality. Forget religion. It's far too structured to suit riding and has been proven to reveal man's inhumanity.*

Christian boldly declared, "My motorcycle is my church. The greatest pew on Earth. Riding is far superior to kneeling."

I liked the man's thinking. We often turn to faith in times of crises when a terrible event disrupts our complacency, leading us to seek answers outside ourselves. Documentaries on prison life show even the most wretched inmates can find solace in God. It seems to work, but when I watch I always think, what about forcing dispicable people to ride motorcycles? Ride until their mindset flips one hundred and eighty degrees or they crash and die.

To the right of Classy sat a Ural with a sidecar. I profiled

Sidecar Guy as probably rereading the Zen book, the one where Buddha metaphorically rides along in the electronics. After introducing himself, he took photos of Classy, saying he'd just finished a three hundred mile camping trip to the northern tip of Vancouver Island. He'd executed a motorcycle triplet: 1) solo rider, 2) camper, 3) on an unusual bike. He went on to lament the Kazakhstan's Ural's warranty service and proudly showcased some of his DIY workarounds.

Top speed? "After eighty kilometers, you're pushing air and draining gas. Beyond its ability to hold too much stuff, I didn't see the point.

Talk about a parking lot one-two punch! Of the dozen bikes waiting to board the ferry, R69S and the Ural were the stars, beating out brand new premium machines; the pair stirred a sense of communal appreciation. I could see it swelling, the glow of Motorcycle Gratitude. Sidecar Guy and I reveled in the infectious joy, delighted to share our treasures, as if we were third graders at show-and-tell. Does this sort of thing happen when golfers swing an old putter or show off a cart with an add-on extra wheel?

As a curious young lad looked over the squadron of bikes, Lady Rider asked the boy about his future dreams.

Without hesitation, the boy exclaimed, "Rocket ship! NASA astronaut," steering our focus from asphalt to the stars.

His appearance, bespectacled and somewhat wimpy looking in his long shorts, made me wonder about his spacefaring aspirations. Would NASA be interested? "Consider zero gravity," I said. "The weightless trainer... they call it the Vomit Comet. Can't compare to the thrill of two wheels."

"Captain Kirk or motorcycle rider?" Lady Rider asked.

The boy thought about the question.

"Aliens or this?" Sidecar Guy's arm swung toward the parked bikes.

A radiant smile illuminated the boy's face, as if he'd won a giant stuffed panda at a carnival. With conviction, he declared, "Motorcycle rider!" his eyes shining with the possibilities of youth.

Welcome to our team, young man.

The ferry's summons rang out, calling the motorbikes to board ahead of the cars and trucks. An orange-vested traffic director gestured us forward. Up the ramp of the Coastal Celebration we went, the sun bathing our procession in a warm glow, each motorcycle a testament to past adventures. A powerful chorus filled the vast parking lot, uniting our group in a camaraderie distinct from those who waited in cages. Classy followed Sidecar Guy onto the upper car deck. I noticed his helmet bobbing as he rode his three-wheeler onto one of the world's largest double-ended ferries. I thought, the Ural hauls a lot of stuff, but doesn't look comfortable.

As the Coastal Celebration heaved its burden away from the dock for the hour and a half, sailing to Vancouver, a text arrived from Marta. All it said was, 'Now it starts for our existential biker.'

Really Marta? Can curmudgeons be existential? Acquaintances would say I value practicality and measurable outcomes and that my straightforwardness is sometimes perceived as bluntness or uncaring. But it has served me well in binary situations.

I seldom consider how I appear to others, as things usually turn out fine. Besides, I have my relief valve. A means to moderate, to avoid becoming annoyed by the insufferable, and god knows there are a lot of those types around. On-motorcycle, you can shrug off intolerable behavior. You realize we're all mere dots traveling through the vastness of the universe. Why sweat the idiots? Anyway, who am I to define acceptable behavior?

In response to Marta's message, I simply sent a thoughtful

emoji: ☺?

◆ ◆ ◆

To avoid distractions from the breaching whale show and the other annoying tourist activities, I settled into a secluded seat and opened the POWER Journal. Ferries are good places to ponder the meaning of it all because you're trapped and there's nothing you can do about it.

Always On

"Always on," I remind riders. Stay sharp by letting extraneous thoughts go—be Always On. It's about riding in the moment, constantly scanning and anticipating, consciously embracing the here and now. An Always On mindset wards off complacency. It puts you in an elevated state of mind. Without it, it's easy to drift off and simply ride, not taking advantage of your extraordinary circumstances. Think about the tools meditators have at their disposal for their assault on enlightenment. Then consider how remarkable your journey on two wheels is.

I mentally ticked a box. There are times I must prod myself, but generally, I'm mostly alert when I ride. Strategies are key for long distance riders, like simply reminding yourself to be Always On. Yelling or singing out loud work for me. Standing on foot pegs, if you have them, or rocking your bike also works. Vary your speed. Or best of all, stop and step off. Use Legs and go for a short walk.

When car drivers pass motorcycles rolling down Nothingness Highway, they think, 'That looks so cool, so liberating, the ultimate freedom.' It's all about perspective. If you're trapped in a cage, going endlessly straight across a vast prairie, riding a motorcycle, looks appealing. NimRods don't know we're grinding it out, repeating to ourselves "Always On," hoping to stay the hell out of Complacency Swamp.

As the Coastal Celebration headed toward the continent, I continued reading the entry, 'Always On.'

...Always On

Motorcycling embodies a duality: part soldier, part yoga master. Despite calm and peaceful surroundings, the threat of assault from any direction is ever-present. That's why commanders instill discipline in soldiers. They constantly gather intelligence, preparing for changing circumstances. As it is for riders, peace is the objective, but there are no guarantees.

Always anticipate. Embrace the movement, feel the wind, remain centered in a state you control, free from imperfections, self-doubts, or failures. Then move beyond that state.

To seasoned riders, Smarty Marty's expressions might seem gimmicky, but simple phrases like 'Now it starts' and 'Always On' stick in one's mind. I gave them both two thumbs up.

As we prepared to leave the ferry's upper deck, a young man, who had shown interest in Classy, voiced his frustrations. He passionately longed for a respectable bike, bemoaning the sorry condition of his "pathetic excuse for a ride." Yearning for a lengthy road trip, he lamented, "it's impossible with this piece of junk." His plight was indeed unfortunate. Furthermore, the young man's discontent stretched beyond his sketchy machine. He griped about the Coastal Celebration's tediously slow docking process and the cafeteria's overpriced subpar food. His attitude stood in sharp contrast to the typical resilience and humor prevalent among riders who most often meet challenges with good-natured fortitude.

Whiner's litany of complaints highlighted a common theme in motorcycle culture: the quest for the ideal machine. It's a common passion that binds us, turning motorcycle frustrations into engaging tales and making folks on lesser bikes envious of those of us on ultimate machines.

"Actually, it's not such a bad bike," I assured the young man. "I've owned worse. A little effort and you'll be on your way." Personally, I'd have ridden his hunk of junk over the rails into the Pacific Ocean. Repeating a line from the journal, I said, "It's not just about the ride, it's about the adventure and the stories created along the way."

"I want one like those." Whiner gestured towards the other bikes on the ferry.

"Believe me, your bike can deliver just as much fun as any of these," I encouraged, using my Gearhead Gandhi voice.

Casting a contemptuous glance my way, Whiner walked off, seemingly in search of someone with real solutions. "Now it starts," I called after him, though the noise of the Coastal Celebration drowned out my words. Whiner spent a few minutes complaining to Sidecar Guy about not having proper camping gear.

Whiner's bike groaned loudly as he revved the engine. But in my mirror, I saw him roll down the ramp and continue his journey. When he passed me in the fast lane, bent over and hugging the bars, I understood why he coveted my machine. A few minutes later, Classy eased by Whiner and left his piece of junk struggling to keep up.

Then Classy turned toward the Peace Arch border crossing, as if it instinctively knew its way home. For me, the only requirement was to maintain discipline. I tucked behind a fast-moving Tesla with a roof rack with what looked like camping gear strapped to it. Mentally, I added a camping note to be shared with Smarty Marty.

Motorcycle Camping Feedback: Is four-wheel camping better than two? In a car, you can haul lots of stuff to be used to mask the reality of camping.

◆ ◆ ◆

Classy and I crossed into the United States of America. Surprisingly, the border guard didn't pose questions like 'Why does your bike have California plates?' 'What's in your bag?' 'You're not the registered owner?' Maybe he was thinking, 'what's the point given the leaky southern border?'

In any case, I was met with a metaphorical 'Welcome to the United States! Your campground awaits, sir'—a sentiment imparted by the wind in the land of the free, not by sentries standing guard.

Peering into the windows of cars and trucks I passed on the interstate, I tried not to gloat. Sure, it's a freeway, but look at me. Riding a classic. Doing the two-wheel boogie.

My hand eased back on the throttle, mindful that on the I5, traffic cops look for out-of-state plates. But I couldn't hold my speed in check for long. Anyway, I was on a classic, riding with a history allowance.

CHAPTER 11 - SOUTH

Among the riders on the interstate that day, I stood out as the only camping enthusiast. Another note to share with Marty:

Motorcycle Camping Feedback: If motorcycle camping is as amazing as Manny and Sidecar Guy suggest, why am I not seeing riders hauling tents and sleeping bags?

At the ferry, I'd spotted a lawn chair atop the Ural's sidecar and asked, "Do you always carry this much stuff? Pretty much your entire house?" Patting my dry bag, I quipped, "Just the essentials for me," as if I were a veteran survivalist who needed little more than his wits.

Sidecar Guy adamantly asserted that every piece of gear was necessary for a civilized experience. "Indispensable," he declared, a grumble of righteous indignation punctuating his tone. "My intention is not to wait the night out and then bugger off at first light." I got the message—he was in the majors; I was a dry bag camping weenie.

Motorcycle Camping Feedback: Serious campers strap on multiple bags, pull trailers, or attach sidecars in order to tote their collection of micro gear with them. Weenies are easy to spot. They have a single bag, one intended to carry sports or beach gear.

Keen to tick camping off my list of mandatory to-dos, I'd programmed my GPS with a few state park destinations. My strategy was straightforward: if the first night was enjoyable, or at least tolerable and financially attractive, I'd add additional stops.

My Smarty Marty notes were piling up:

<u>Motorcycle Camping Feedback</u>: Camping is a money saver, providing the freedom to roll farther down the endless highway.

Manny argues, 'it's about connecting with nature, not cutting costs."

Really, Manny? When you go camping, don't forget to give me the dollars you saved by not staying in motels.

In the early afternoon, SatNav guided me onto a scenic country road that would lead me to Highway 2. I turned left, passed through a traffic light, and entered one of those meandering roads that had been seamlessly integrated into nature's design. The traffic was light, and Mother Nature had done a stellar job on both sides of the road.

Ever seen those 'Freedom' posters featuring a motorcycle? Imagine Leonardo da Vinci or Vincent van Gogh capturing the essence of two-wheeled freedom on canvas. I was experiencing just that, in control of my destiny, free from the need to please, placate, or argue with anyone. On a perfect machine, one curve slicing into the next.

'You can't buy happiness, but you can buy a motorcycle.' Those are the type of words you see on motorcycle posters. Or 'Never Stop Exploring.' 'Two Wheels Move The Soul.' 'Chase Horizons.' The words are usually better than the artwork. 'Motorcycle on Velvet', which hangs in my garage, doesn't have a slogan.

For two hours, I traveled on the country road, traversing a tiny speck of our vast galaxy. I found myself alone; no other motorcycles. Not that it mattered, because every person is on their own existential quest.

Note On Riding Solo: Embracing solitude is a journey unto itself.

My tranquility was jolted when a dilapidated pickup swung wide in a corner. "Asshole!" slipped out as an instinctive response, though in fairness, the driver barely lost control. Thinking of a story Smarty Marty told, I shrugged off the incident as if it were a bug glancing off my visor.

A man asks Bob, "I'm thinking of joining your group; what's your take on the people and community here?"

"How do you find the people where you currently hang out?"

The newcomer replies, "A bunch of egotistical, mean-spirited, spiteful assholes."

Bob then answers the original question, "Then you'll find the people here assholes, too. Best not join."

Later, another man poses the same question to Bob: "I'm interested in joining your group. How are the people and community here?"

"What are the people like where you are now?"

The newcomer replies, "They're kind-hearted, considerate people. Smart as well. I've enjoyed hanging out with them."

Bob answers, "The people here are the same; you'll enjoy their company."

In the journal Smarty Marty explains, "In the story, the only thing that made Bob's response change was the newcomer's perspective. If you believe the world is filled with assholes, you'll encounter them everywhere. Your bike can be used as a tool to reshape your perspective. Work not only on riding, but mastering your emotions, thoughts, and reactions. In this changing world, you are what remains constant. There will be rough days and sour moods. We can't control everything, but we can choose our response. Riding forces you to take charge, to not be a passive traveler. Use the discipline learned from riding to calm your emotions and control your perspective."

So I practiced the art of letting go. I wished the pickup driver well. After all, his truck was in worse shape than Whiner's motorcycle.

◆ ◆ ◆

On Country Road, a place where exhilarating moments intertwine with tranquility, I suddenly felt overwhelmed. Panic took hold, but miraculously, just as I teetered on the brink of exploding, the forest cleared, like the parting of the Red Sea. In front of me was a perfect pullover—Lake Roesiger County Park, featuring a fully functional washroom in front of a pretty lake. It's unfathomable how things fall into place.

Caught up in my haste to avoid a messy situation, I neglected to review the regulations and inadvertently violated a Snohomish County parking bylaw. There were no picnickers, waders, lovers, hikers, homeless campers, drug addicts, or enforcers about, so my snub went unchallenged.

Motorcycle freedom doesn't extend to biological functions— when nature calls, you gotta go.

Classy remained on the roadway in front of the concrete block restroom. Sure, I was a parking violator, but the people-in-charge of signage like to make up dumb rules. It wouldn't have bothered Richard Roesiger, a German immigrant and one of the first non-native residents of the region. A kinship exists between historical explorers and modern-day adventurers. Pioneers left their birthplaces to escape repression and make their own rules, just as bikers 'get out of Dodge' today in order to escape the news and political noise.

As I walked away from the restroom, the tranquility of the lake water brought a profound sense of calm. Or perhaps it was empty bladder relief? In my moment of need, it appeared the universe had provided. Admittedly, Snohomish County had also been involved.

It's often the case when you ride, you get to where you need to be. The inexplicable nature of these events hints at a grander design.

Brimming with gratitude, I settled on a bench to absorb the beauty before me. Surrounded by nature's splendor, I felt assured of a flawless journey. The bench was spartan and uncomfortable, so I soon rose and strolled over to the information board.

I learned that Richard Roesiger had advertised, "looking for a wife who can milk a cow." In contrast, modern dating apps don't prioritize practical skills. You won't find profiles stating, "seeking a partner who can fix a flat."

It leaves one wondering how things turned out for Richard. Was he content with his choice, or did he eventually think, 'Perhaps milking cows myself wasn't a bad way to go?'

We're all looking for that person who can milk cows while being our soul mate.

Note On Riding Solo: Finding an ideal riding companion is difficult. One who matches your skill, speed, endurance, and temperament.

Another Lake Roesiger County Park regulation: dogs must be on a leash. I was sure that Richard didn't walk around with his dog leashed, and if Pearly had been with me, she'd be under control but not leashed. In Richard's honor, I gave that regulation the biker salute.

Littering is strictly prohibited in Lake Roesiger County Park. The issue arises because cagers carry tons of crap with them. I gave **No Littering** a thumbs up.

"Glaciers advancing down the foothills of the Cascade Mountains formed Lake Roesiger, the largest of 463 lakes in the area. The melting ice left behind large bodies of water," the sign informed me.

Really? I imagined the story unfolding on public television, with stuffed shirt scholars offering insights as though they had personally witnessed the event. I prefer Mr. Roesiger's straightforward approach. Practical skills are crucial for both homesteading and motorcycling.

I grabbed a mango-peach flavored water drink, along with trail mix, and returned to sit on the bench facing the waves. *What percentage of the lake water originated from melted ice?* If I had a wetsuit, and the water was warmer by twenty degrees, and if I'd been the star of the high school swim team, I'd definitely have dived in. As the wind does, water has the power to change your perspective, forcing you to be present. God knows what the glaciers deposited in the muddy depths of Lake Roesiger? It would be beautiful, calming, otherworldly, and terrifying all at once at the bottom of the lake. Bloodsuckers may attack, but no need to worry about deranged stags.

If Sidecar Guy were here, he'd probably be lounging on the lake with his air mattress and pool cup.

Motorcycle Camping Feedback: Is skinny dipping the norm for minimalist solo campers?

Although swimming and motorcycle riding share similarities, there is one insurmountable obstacle that cannot be overcome: water, water everywhere. We're not blubbering whales! Humans can't float endlessly or stay submerged for an hour.

I concluded waves could never replace the therapeutic experience of the wind. It may be why I prefer hot tubs and Hanauma Bay to cold water lakes.

I grabbed a handful of trail mix and pondered mindful eating. This is yet another self-help strategy that has never proven effective for me. The idea is to differentiate between physical and emotional hunger. Gazing at my snack, I asked, how does this food make me feel? I already knew it made me feel like picking out all the yogurt-covered cranberries.

Mindful eating falls far short in its ability to reduce caloric intake when compared to restricting food by riding a motorcycle. The problem occurs when one steps off, often in front of a coffee shop or a fast-food joint.

Seeking a distraction from mindlessly eating all the yogurt cranberries, I turned to Smarty Marty's journal.

A Jolt

Think of riding a motorcycle as mindfulness revved up. Riders embark on a journey of heightened consciousness, far removed from the idle thoughts of cross-legged meditation but moving faster toward the pursuit of enlightenment. The motorcycle seat transforms into a meditation mat, offering a jolt of visceral experience that resonates deep within.

For most riders, motorcycle mindfulness begins automatically, as concentration and total awareness are imperatives.

The moment you climb on, your senses are engulfed in an ever-shifting tapestry of sights and sounds. You feel the bike's pulse, hear its rumble, and take in the world around you. Accept two-wheel awareness and the stage is set for a deeper connection.

Mindfulness gurus suggest techniques like gazing up at the sky or listening to meditative music to help students grasp the esoteric nature of their practice. In contrast, the criteria for motorcycle mindfulness is simple—if you can feel the wind, you're on the right path.

The journey starts with an initial jolt that reverberates through your core, linking you to the extraordinary synergy of man, machine, and exploration. As you exclaim, 'I'm alive!' you progress and come to understand that it's not just a ride; it's a wake-up call wrapped in movement.

As Classy turned left onto Highway 2, my attention was drawn to an alien presence—an intruder—an unusual patch of green, not the expected indigenous shade, but something foreign. It shone, not unlike a lone neon sign in a sleepy town, standing out like a chopper gearing up for an attempt at the local hill climb.

It was a large bamboo plantation. Alongside the grove was a pullout, but I didn't stop. On the opposite side of the two-lane highway sat 'The Reptile Zoo', displaying an open sign. The bamboo forest likely served as an open range breeding ground for the reptile business.

I wondered if the attraction had interactive elements like the petting zoo at Beacon Hill Park with its goats. The Reptile Zoo boasted a two-headed turtle, but I was too early for the snake feeding event (5:30 to 7 PM). There was an extra fee to see snakes devouring rodents. The zoo invited me to adopt a reptile and contribute to its ongoing care and feeding.

A good number of cars waited in the zoo parking lot. Not a single motorbike in sight.

Note on Riding Solo: If you had to pair up, would you prefer a snake lover or a badass motorcycle gang member?

Dogs wearing goggles, riding in sidecars, exude an unmistakable joy. Back at the Swartz Bay ferry terminal, Sidecar Guy told me he'd love the companionship of a dog, but mutts weren't permitted where he lived. Should we meet again, I'll ask, 'How 'bout a boa constrictor or a reticulated python? You won't have to worry about theft, and your snake can feed on small pets while you sleep.' I know. I know. It'd be repulsive to disrespect a motorcycle by allowing a snake to wrap itself around the handlebar.

Families in cars, especially those with kids, are often drawn to stops like reptile zoos, particularly those boasting a rare two-headed freak. They also enjoy water and adventure parks with ice cream parlors. On-motorcycle, the road is your stage; there's no need to stop at tourist sideshows.

Stopping, of course, remains a necessity, chiefly the need for restroom breaks. A sign declared **Historical Site Ahead**. Without the prospect of a two-headed turtle or free coffee, cars sped by. So, I pulled over onto the gravel and discreetly relieved myself, then examined the sign. It had something to do with a barely visible large boulder which had no doubt been deposited by the same glacier that formed Lake Roesiger. The attraction was underwhelming but, if Historical Sites were compelling and swarming with tourists, they wouldn't be viable pee stops.

As I resumed my journey, the road seemed to have a defiant streak etched into its pale asphalt, challenging me. I complied until a traffic cop waved me over.

Only fourteen over on a straightaway entrapment zone, not bad. The radar gun was the sole reason to moderate my speed.

"Your license and registration." The young officer requested, as if I had a choice.

Keep your mouth shut, Marta's advice played in my mind. I got off Classy, unstrapped my dry bag, and pulled the seat off to retrieve Martin's registration. I handed it, along with my license, to the officer, who quickly noticed the mismatch between the license name and the registration.

"You're not the owner? What brings you here?"

It was a big question. What are any of us doing here? A question best left unanswered in such situations. "A friend lent me his bike. He volunteers with a therapeutic riding group... military, law enforcement, and others folks. I help out a bit." The officer looked doubtful. "I have a letter from the owner, a video, and his phone number."

The cop tilted his head and squinted, trying to size me up. Was I being deceitful? Holding Martin's letter, he instructed, "Wait by the bike."

Note On Riding Solo: There are circumstances that make lone riders think 'it'd sure be great to have a companion.' A mechanic for emergency repairs or a blonde bombshell able to charm cops and avoid minor tickets.

As the cop spoke, I felt a twinge of Motorcycle Gratitude. "Watch your speed. Be a real shame if anything happened to your classic."

I donned my 'sincerely grateful smile.'

"Or you," the officer added. The young man shared that he was an off-roader planning a road trip "one of these years." He asked if I'd mind taking a picture of him beside the R69, a request I happily obliged.

Unexpectedly, I'd met a roadside Motorcycle Friend. You never know.

CHAPTER 12 - OVER
THE MOUNTAINS

For those seeking the thrill of untamed nights, the Cascade Mountains hold a treasure trove of secluded camping spots. Bypass the registration process—why dole out hard-earned cash to sleep on the ground? Upscale your engine oil instead. Establish your camp in the traditional territories of the Duwamish, Snohomish, Snoqualmie, Skagit, Suiattle, Samish, and Stillaguamish peoples, as Richard Roesiger did in 1882. Dick overlooked ancestral rights and land use rigmarole, yet now, a pleasant park and a glacial lake stand as testaments to his legacy.

<u>Motorcycle Camping Feedback:</u> Embrace your primal instincts. Forget manicured campgrounds; just you, your motorcycle, and nature alone in the wilderness.

We ascended, climbing through the thinning, cooler air towards towering mountain vistas, with the road unraveling before us like a ribbon to the sky. Classy accelerated out of an uphill curve, then eased into a straight stretch where I slowed to marvel at the spectacle.

The fragrance of nature, carried by a gentle breeze, hung in the air, each breath serving as a reminder of my reality—there was only now. With small green meadows, wildflowers, granite, and a majestic sky, the wilderness resembled a Monet painting. The sun's rays seemed to bring the colors to life, beckoning me to choose a camping spot. 'Anywhere you fancy, Mike. You're welcome here.'

Motorcycle Camping Feedback: Camping gear provides accommodation insurance. Your tent is your castle, granting you the autonomy to bed down anytime, anywhere.

Reaching the summit of Stevens Pass, the air grew cooler, and misty clouds covered the landscape with a veil. It was as if Mother Nature had drawn her curtain. Undaunted, Classy and I began our descent down the east slope, excited to reach a Thrilling Ride detour SatNav had mapped out not far away.

The curvy road wandered around the north side of Lake Wenatchee at close to 2000ft above sea level. I'm pretty good at painting sweepers. As basketball legend Larry Bird said about mastering shooting, "I now know where on the court I can take my shots." The learning comes in chunks, gradually forming a complete understanding. It's like getting a book of chords when you're fourteen. At first you make a god awful racket, but keep practicing and you'll hear your inner rock star emerge. With motorcycles, we feel a bit of MottoGP emerge.

The hum of the engine and the sound of the wind provided my soundtrack, accompanying me as I guided Classy through each turn, my senses intensifying, Classy responding to the slightest weight on the bars. I relished this tactile connection, feeling the engine beneath me and the texture of the grips under my gloves. Every change in the asphalt, every nuance of movement resonated through my body, inviting me to scrape my pegs.

For the R69, it was effortless. Classy easily mastered everything in its path. The bike's combination of style, elegance, and comfort made me feel like I could sink my shots, aware of my boundaries.

Note on Riding Solo: Each throttle twist and body shift is a conversation with the road, a salute to freedom composed by the rider. Each rider is a commander, playing their game like Larry Bird.

At a point where the Thrilling Ride seemed like it should flow uninterrupted, a stop sign appeared.

'All Things Must Pass,' George Harrison sang—but why must it be so? Classy rolled to a stop on the deserted road.

At the point Lake Wenatchee Road intersects Highway 2 sits Lake Wenatchee State Park. "Campsites, plenty of trails, a beautiful lake. The perfect spot," I announced when I accepted my challenge at Tony's bistro. "For my return to camping." I imagined dipping my toe in icy lake water, a symbolic gesture celebrating my return to the world of camping.

"Expansive," Manny had said, referring to the park's 492 acres. "There's a lot to see. You won't be bored."

Whatever, Manny. You didn't notice? It's mostly trees and water.

"Wanna bet?" Conrad had asked.

Upon reaching the turnoff for the park, I hesitated as clouds shrouded much of it. Ultimately, I opted not to make the turn. Enduring bad weather on a bike can be miserable, but sheltering inside a tent going nowhere is self-imposed torture. To be honest, the conditions weren't dire. Meteorologists would have described the weather as: 'slightly shitty with clearing later in the day.' Nonetheless, I was unwilling to compromise my camping comeback.

Motorcycle Camping Feedback: Camping wisdom includes knowing when to seek the shelter of a motel over battling the elements in a flimsy tent.

As I descended the eastern slope, a change in the weather breathed new life into my ambitions. I'd selected a backup site near the city of Wenatchee. I'd have to bend my 'stop early, leave late rule,' but adaptability is vital when touring.

Anticipation grew as I imagined disembarking to pitch my tent. Then I'd take a selfie and report, 'Mission accomplished! I am a motorcycle camper!'

◆ ◆ ◆

Nestled in the embrace of two rivers lies Wenatchee Confluence State Park. Wanting to lighten the reality of camping with snakes, I imagined Mickey and Minnie Mouse moving to the park's nature sanctuary, only to find themselves stalked by hungry reptiles. It'd make a great National Geographic documentary, especially if the dilemma was resolved by the couple finding a pair of tiddlers, pulling wheelies, and fleeing back to the safety of Disneyland.

Motorcycle Camping Feedback: Motel rooms don't have snakes.

Manny told me about a ten-mile hiking loop along the Columbia River. "Stayed three nights at Confluence to see everything."

Really, Manny? Did you also start a fire with a stick and roast rattlers?

Approaching the park on Classy, a nagging rookie worry struck me—had I forgotten something crucial? Like the rod that holds the tent up?

Motorcycle Camping Feedback: Expert campers often rely on meticulous checklists and packing rituals, similar to those used by secretive societies like the Free Masons.

Anticipating unexpected challenges, I had stocked R69's toolkit with the essentials: a multi-tool, zip ties, and duct tape.

Note On Riding Solo: When you've ridden too long, it's hot as hell, and your brain's numbing, solo riders often wish they were following a lead rider, one who's an expert at sorting things out.

The moment SatNav signaled my upcoming exit, I was overwhelmed by a deluge of signs and speeding vehicles, making it impossible to process the information barrage.

Road Construction

Detour

No Access to Easy Street

Use Alternate Exit

As I attempted to unravel the maze, my patience blew a gasket. My GPS, ignoring the warnings, stubbornly clung to its original plan. All the while, rush hour traffic screamed at me, 'No dawdling—keep moving, biker boy.'

My feedback generator was pissed. Martin, if the present moment is chaos, you don't want to be in it!

I throttled up, slowed, and turned off at the next exit. Frustrated by the frantic GPS recalculations, I pulled over to regroup. SatNav remained firm about returning to the freeway and taking the barricaded park exit. The combination of chaos and sweltering heat rendered a clear verdict: the night was not meant for camping. "Fuck it," I said. I'd already missed my stop early deadline. Time for Plan B.

Motorcycle Camping Feedback: Motels scream for attention, but campsites prefer to portray an air of mystery, often tucked away in secluded spots. Places like the dead-end road to Dog Creek or at the bottom of Rattlesnake Gulch. Conversely, motels flaunt their presence with gigantic signs on main streets proclaiming 'Welcome' and 'Vacancy,' openly vying for traveler's attention.

Note On Riding Solo: In a group, responsibility is shared and individual screw ups are lost in the crowd. But solo? The buck stops with you.

Finally, SatNav's guidance made sense: 'No worries, I've got a nice motel lined up for you. Follow my directions.' Classy wheeled around and rolled toward town.

Note On Riding Solo: In a group ride, changing the plan can spark heated debates. Solo decisions are swift and unchallenged.

"Survive to camp another day," Conrad says. "Stay in motels."
Carrying camping gear to my motel came with a drawback: it must be unload or I'd risk losing it to homeless urban campers.

Motorcycle Camping Feedback: Handling unused gear offers an excellent opportunity to mingle with travelers in motel parking lots.

Settled in my room, I began the ritual of unwinding from the day's journey. I removed my riding gear, turned on the AC, grabbed a complimentary bottle of water, and arranged the pillows. Then I lay on the bed and opened the POWER Journal.

Is it Time to Shop?

Do you ever feel like you're not reaching your full potential? You're not alone. Wellness and enlightenment are overwhelmingly complex. Medical science progresses, but we continue to face a relentless array of challenges. We can't escape life's bombardments. Gossip mongering. Cancellation culture. Fake news. Trolls. Politicians. Influencers. Bosses. UN declarations and all the other noise makers and takers.

Innovators attempt to bridge the gap between medical science and holistic health by offering ways to rise above it all. They sell hope and remediation for some, but for others, their remedies fall short.

Why not skip the self-help aisle and go directly to the motorcycle store? Where else can you shop for balance? Follow the motorcycle prescription and ride away. Does that not make more sense than buying essential oils to use in a heal thyself ceremony?

Allow yourself to be selfish. Change the channel. Buy a motorcycle.

I gave Smarty Marty's words a mental check mark. Putting a down payment on a bike makes a lot of sense. Marta would say, "We only have the power to change between birth and death and you're not dead! So get moving!"

CHAPTER 13 - THE MYSTERIOUS EAST

So often we live with regrets over past choices—like bailing on the Baja trip, trusting an old battery, or slavishly following mundane routines. These "what-ifs" etch themselves in our memories, deepening with each missed opportunity. Then along comes a catalyst, perhaps a move, or a traumatic event, or a relationship, that rejuvenates our spirit. In the aftermath of going down hard, my life lens changed.

It's not that I jumped out of bed in my Wenatchee motel, brimming with song and dance; I simply continued my journey. As I drew the blinds and saw Classy standing in the morning light, I felt blessed. Is Martin an honest-to-God motorcycle saint? They're out there, on the roads and in coffee shops.

With a sip of my coffee, I opened the POWER journal, in a mood to delve into the thoughts of Martin Holmes.

Escape Pods

Our brains navigate us through life, trying to steer us toward fulfillment. We begin as blank slates, only to learn about things like regret, doubt, betrayal, hostility, and brutality as well as love and appreciation. We learn we should be attractive but are never attractive enough. Aiming to be smart, we act foolishly. Aspiring to be wealthy, we often find ourselves squandering money. Faced with infinite possibilities, we succumb to the constraints of what we are taught.

How can we escape this conditioning? How do we unshackle ourselves? Change the channel? Where can we go to unlearn our lessons? Perhaps we need a vacation? But that page is quickly turned and we're back where we began. How about starting a new regimen? But perseverance is fleeting. Drugs, initially an ally, soon turn against us. There is faith, but even Mother Teresa had doubts.

Our brains are exposed to incessant feedback loops that fuel human perceptions. We need to break the cycle. Is there a more disruptive tool than motorcycles? They can be liberation machines moving us away from what we've been taught and closer to what Buddhists call the 'original mind,' the time before our first thought, before life began to teach us its ways.

I found myself drawn back to the window, admiring my escape pod. I've always formed relationships with the bikes I've owned. Like human relationships, some resonated deeply, while others were forgettable or even bothersome.

It was an insight worth sharing, so I recorded a feedback message: "Martin, consider discussing the importance of owning a compatible bike. If size, power, style, or some other aspect makes a rider uncomfortable, it'll impede their escape. As Marta suggests, 'Every rider needs a union of trust.'"

As I was leaving to strap my dry bag on, a text arrived. I put my gear on the bed and read Marta's note: 'How was your first night camping? Any snakes?'

At first, I typed out, 'It was f'ing great,' but after a moment of reflection, I chose a simpler response: 'Awesome, what an escape.'

Marta can always tell when I'm bullshitting.

While adjusting a tie-down strap, I caught sight of a heavyset woman heading toward a mid-sized cruiser. As she spun around, coffee cascaded over the edge of her mug. "Shit!" I heard as she frowned. Then she tucked a dust rag into her jacket pocket and approached.

A biker in distress… about to request a favor I'd rather avoid? I was eager to leave in peace, but the robust woman's expression made me suspect she was about to impose.

She smiled before saying, "Good morning. Couldn't help but admire your bike. A beauty. What year?" The lady had a warm, cuddly voice, what you'd expect from a fat person.

Relieved, I answered, "63."

She bombarded me with insightful questions and soon we were lost in an admiration session. "My dad owned a '73 Electra-Glide. The first bike I rode. Dad ran along beside, terrified I'd damage his pride and joy." Then the lady introduced herself as "Large Marge."

Tipping the scales over two hundred pounds, I guessed. Her clothes said, I'm a motorcycle mamma.

"Too small for me," Large Marge said, seriously. "Had to upgrade the shocks on my bad boy." She pointed toward her bike and, following a classic motorcycle script, shared that she was riding to Yellowstone to make a fresh start after a tough breakup. "He's a fat slob of a man. We both enjoy food too much," she laughed. "I miss the big lug."

It was evident Large Marge's journey hadn't yet been long enough to soothe her heartache. She hadn't discarded her emotional trash. "I keep telling myself I'm leaving him in the dust." She finished her coffee with a slurp and said, "Still a way to go."

Note On Riding Solo: Motorcycles are often used to escape bad relationships. Ride away, alone, to start over is a classic story. In books, it always works great.

Feeling it might be my destiny, I felt I had to say something.

"Been reading my friend's notes. He leads therapeutic riding programs. It's all about the power of motorcycles to do good."

Large Marge nodded, but otherwise didn't respond.

"I've always felt there was something to wind therapy. My friend dived right in."

Again Marge nodded. After a moment, she said, "Never really thought seriously about it." Her body jiggled as she rubbed her forehead. "Boy, do I need some good." She coughed out a belly laugh. "Bit of a mess, here." She pointed toward herself.

"Now it starts. That's what they say to get members in the right frame of mind. Give it a try... so you're not just traveling toward Yellowstone full of relationship regrets. Ride with an open mind and stay in the moment." As we talked about therapeutic riding, and as I listened to Marge reveal the urgency she felt to change, I emailed excerpts from the POWER journal. "Read a few before you leave. They'll help put things in perspective."

I received an emotional thank you. Then Large Marge quoted a line from a poem, "Be glad and your friends are many." She continued, "I'm looking forward to reading your friend's thoughts. Now it starts!"

In another world, where our outlaw personas didn't dictate our actions and one of us wasn't notably obese with enormous breasts, we might have parted with a hug.

Before leaving the motel, I sent Martin a picture of Large Marge standing beside Classy captioning it, "a work in progress." As I pocketed my phone, I pictured Marge sitting in her room, reading parts of the journal. Soon she'd head toward Yellowstone, hopefully armed with the motorcycle prescription.

As Classy rolled out of the parking lot, I found myself humming *When You're Smiling.*

<u>Note on Riding Solo</u>: The perfect anthem for a solo journey? 'Only The Lonely'? 'Owner of a Lonely Heart'? No! Belt out 'You'll Never Walk Alone' or 'Laugh and the World Laughs with You.' Or simply listen to the symphony of the road.

Singing "Get your motor running, head out on the highway," I guided Classy past the barricaded Wenatchee Confluence State Park exit. We were chasing the rising sun.

I patted my dry bag, assuring it, "Tonight's, the night."

<u>Motorcycle Camping Feedback</u>: Carrying camping gear is like bringing a tire repair kit. No room at the inn? No worries. I'll use my safety net.

If today's planners had their way, they'd use heavy equipment to iron Highway 2 across Washington state's central plain, straightening and flattening its irregularities. Their justification would be 'we're paving the way for autonomous driving and don't give a shit about motorcycles.'

Thankfully, the asphalt was laid down before today's total disregard for the lay of the land took hold. East of Wenatchee, travelers are greeted by peaceful, scenic landscapes filled with rolling hills and gentle curves, delivering enough variation to evade those doldrums of monotony that drown riders in Complacency Swamp. But save your fortitude, you'll need to use some of it further east.

It's magical, riding toward the sun, low in a vibrant morning sky, at a time and angle where the rays aren't blinding you. It's rare and it's a gratitude filler.

The peace was intermittently broken by light traffic, like the click of a channel change. In my motel room, I'd foolishly tuned in to catch up on current events. The world, as depicted on the screen, was grim. The reality surrounding me on-motorcycle painted the opposite picture.

A truth about motorcycles: motorcycles have the power to change the channel.

As the landscape merged with my thoughts, the absurdities of the world faded into irrelevance. If only there was a way to package those moments as feedback. Marty, here is the power of motorcycles on display. Show your community; words are not necessary.

No other mechanism can do the job. Cars lock the wind and nature out, trapping bad news inside. Bicycling demands a Herculean effort to break free of humanity's constant barrage. Golf is a breeding ground for frustration. Only the two-wheel boogie will do. With my visor up, I tilted my head, letting the air touch my cheek. "It's a beautiful morning," I sang. "The sun is shining everywhere."

There I was, in central Washington State, immersed in the enlightenment others seek from mystics in remote corners of the world. The secret? I was sitting on a motorcycle, not under a Bodhi tree.

The landscape unfolding before me revealed an array of idyllic camping spots. 'Take your pick,' nature called, tempting me to stop my journey prematurely. I continued eastward.

Motorcycle Camping Feedback: The diversity of campsites, in contrast to the uniformity of motel rooms, often leads riders to ponder, 'what if there's a better spot down the road?

Or perhaps I'll pass by an amazing motel offer?

<u>Motorcycle Camping Feedback</u>: The rustic charms of the great outdoors compete with the mental imagery of cozy motel rooms.

Highway 2 offered a calming rhythm, neither aggressive nor bland, striking a balance, reminiscent of a well-lived life, neither lethargic nor excessive. The road was a trusted, comfortable companion.

In these parts, sweepers are cherished. I hugged the tank with my knees, bent forward at the waist, and flexed my core like a racer, using smoothness to enable more speed. Then, on straightaways, I slowed to avoid attracting the attention of law enforcement and their NimRod informants. *Mr. and Mrs. Sedan here. One of those horrible bikers just blasted by us. Yes, definitely more than eleven over.*

To stay within the forgiveness zone, I throttled my speed, releasing it on curves where radar guns are seldom drawn.

I don't always ride smoothly. At least once per riding season a distraction or the unforeseen scares the bejesus out of me. It's not like golf where you cheat or take a mulligan. On-motorcycle you shake your head and thank your muscle memory.

Further east, Highway 2 follows the natural terrain, which is unvarying as the doldrums. All there is to see are vast stretches of sagebrush, grazing fields, and deer warning signs. In this area, stags have as much chance of successfully planning an ambush as the Iraqi army did during the Gulf War. A wild turkey may hide in the tall grass, prepared to launch itself like a missile, but I had no fear of kamikaze deer—I'd see them galloping a mile off and shoot the buggers with my pointed finger. *Martin, if you have members plagued by agrizoophobia (the fear of wild animal attacks), encourage them to ride on the plains.*

In a realm beyond monotony, riders engage in a silent

duel with the mundane as it attempts to strangle situational awareness. Martin addressed this condition in the POWER Journal. One of his tips is this: focus on a distant vehicle or a structure. Turn them into objects of fascination. Concentrate on the entity without diminishing your situational awareness. Invent questions and answers for all possible inquiries about the object. It's the motorcycle equivalent of focused breathing, but way more fun.

I targeted a speck in the distance. I guessed the make and model of the oncoming vehicle. Next the year, color, destination, number of occupants along with a story about their circumstances. As the sedan revealed itself and passed, I awarded myself a B+. Next was a transport truck. I suspected the driver was in the human smuggling business hauling a load of sex slaves. I had half a mind to follow, but my attention was diverted by a suspicious building that had emerged on the horizon.

A sign proclaimed **City Center,** but the scene was a stark contradiction. Absent were towering high-rises, loud noises, and urban chaos. It was like a ghost town. No litter swirled in the breeze nor were there sirens, wailing distress calls.

In need of both coffee and gas, I'd turned Classy to the right to bring us into the city center. 'Welcome! Here everything is under control,' seemed to be the unspoken message. Downtown Coulee City is a modest two-block strip of unobtrusive buildings.

Not a wheel stirred, except for Classy's, but a sudden and unexpected interaction was about to unfold. As I swung around to head back to Highway 2, the abrupt emergence of a man frantically waving in the middle of Main Street disrupted the stillness, sparking both alarm and curiosity. I checked— everything about the R69 seemed to be fine. Do I zip by him and bugger off, or fall into his city center trap?

The man continued waving and smiling. I wondered: might he be an R69S owner himself? Was it an emergency, or did he want to know if I'd ride my classic in the Coulee City 4th of July parade? Classy eased to a stop in the middle of Main Street beside the gent. I opened my visor. "Yes?"

"Looking for a bite?" asked the man.

Bite? Confused, I switched off the engine to hear clearly. Curious about the man's intentions, I removed my helmet and earplugs, urging him to speak up. *Is he going to offer me a sandwich? Invite me to his home? Or was he flogging stale muffins? Was I about to become another of his victims, misled by the City Center sign?*

"There's not much here."

I nodded—that's for sure. The man resembled a retired grain farmer; salt of the earth with a happiness rooted in the soil. Likely religious and kind-hearted. Five kids, all living in big cities now, one overseas and one with a thrasher injury. Conversation is often one-sided when you're geared up, stopped in the middle of Main Street, and not the initiator of the encounter. I waited, my curiosity mounting, before asking, "What's up?"

"Half a mile. On the south side of the highway. That way." He waved his hand toward the east, his enthusiastic directions a sharp contrast to the silent streets. "Great coffee and food." He seemed quite pleased with himself as he mentioned, "Homemade baked goods."

Silently, I wondered, 'Might you be the owner or the baker?'

"Nice bike," the Coulee City Greeter said, as though he'd flagged down many motorcycles.

"Thanks. I'll check the cafe out." I smiled, slipped my ear plugs into my pocket, and pulled my helmet on.

The stranger gazed contentedly, watching Classy move out of the city center.

◆ ◆ ◆

The lively café, brimming with the scents of freshly brewed coffee and oven-fresh goods, radiated a country welcome. Discreetly, I brushed away what might have been drool from my chin. Creaking floorboards and buzzing conversations contributed to the charm. An enthusiastic woman behind the counter, possibly Greeter's daughter, smiled warmly. "Blueberry," I responded. "Blueberry-lemon actually. Your muffins come highly recommended." *Did your dad bake them?*

After setting my helmet on a counter below the front window, I took a stool with a view of Classy and the parking area. A couple of guys entered and walked directly over to me. "Your bike?"

"The old Beemer," the other added in a friendly way, pointing toward Classy.

I nodded, choosing not to elaborate further.

"Beauty."

The other guy whistled.

And so it started, an R69S admiration session, followed by the announcement, "We'll soon be riding to somewhere in Alaska. We have two weeks. Haven't picked out our finish line yet."

We discussed potential routes, timing, weather, what to bring, and the likelihood of encountering wildlife. The unseasoned travelers were keen on reaching the Arctic Circle —it was their goal. "How about Hyder, on the panhandle?" I suggested. "It's in Alaska and a manageable distance... for a first attempt. The drive in is spectacular. You should ride north from Terrace." Glaciers tower over the highway, while bikes weave along rivers, through ancient forests, and past lava beds. "An incredible trip. And you can cap it off by getting Hyderized, the tradition of downing a shot of 150 proof Everclear alcohol." I shuddered. "Got my certificate."

In a gesture of gratitude, the young men bought me a refill before heading back to work. Naturally, I indulged in a second muffin: strawberry-rhubarb this time. Not under-baked, but pretty damn good. Armed and ready, I opened the POWER Journal.

Your Trainer

As the adage goes, 'There's never a bad day when I'm riding.' You're having a great day, so what do you do? Build gratitude. It'll sustain you.

Gratitude is a mindset: It's as different from being angry as 180 degrees is from zero, as distinct from laziness as 90 degrees is from a flat line, and as separate from frivolity as 60 degrees is from being parallel.

Just like in physical fitness, where every degree of effort counts to build gratitude, every shift in perspective matters. Changes fly at us when we're on the road—absorb and appreciate each one. Just as building muscle requires regular exercise, so does your mind need training to grow stronger, to see the world unclouded by past perceptions and remain in the moment.

Think of your motorcycle as a gratitude trainer, more than just transportation or a way to get a thrill.

Classy turned and began traveling north along Highway 155, hugging the contours of Banks Lake, a sprawling reservoir that stretches for twenty-seven miles. The Coulee City Duo had recommended Steamboat Rock State Park. The campground's online images were appealing. I imagined a welcoming sign that read: **You've Arrived Where You Were Meant To Be.**

But as I drew nearer and considered the practicalities, doubts surfaced. Nearing the crucial decision point, my reservations transformed into outright defiance. "I have limits." Classy surged ahead. I observe 'Stop Early' but the clock had not yet struck one. I wasn't about to spend a substantial amount of time alone at a campsite for the sole purpose of helping Smarty Marty with his pet project.

<u>Motorcycle Camping Feedback</u>: For solo minimalist campers, timing is everything. Arrive too early, and you find yourself sitting on the ground, questioning your choice—what the fuck am I supposed to do now? Too late, and you're frantically setting up in the crappiest spot.

<u>Note On Riding Solo</u>: To communal campers, the sight of a lone rider unloading a case of beer at one o'clock is sad. Party of one.

The Grand Coulee Dam stands as a monument to human ingenuity and its ability to reshape nature; it's the United States' largest power station by rated capacity. "Horsepower matters for both motorcycles and dams," I told Classy. In order to fully absorb the awe-inspiring size and scale of one of the world's largest concrete structures, I detoured into the visitors' center. Inside this engineering wonder, I found the washroom to be functional but unremarkable.

At the urinal next to me, a tourist in Hawaiian shorts remarked, "That's a lot of cement."

"Concrete," I corrected him.

Not put off, he nodded and said, "Beautiful day for a ride, huh?" then zipped. It's a familiar remark. "Doesn't get any better, right?"

He shared his dream of buying a bike post-retirement, sixteen years away. I couldn't resist giving him some advice. "Why wait and miss out on all that time?" *What's wrong with you, mister? Seize the day! ALWAYS ON!*

He gave a noncommittal shrug and looked a little miffed.

I'd be a homeless camper if I relied on motivational speaking to make my living.

◆ ◆ ◆

I continued my journey, heading southeast on 174 until it merged back onto Highway 2. An hour later, Classy turned onto a less-traveled road, one SatNav promised would offer a thrilling ride. It didn't disappoint.

Fresh black asphalt snaked through glorious twists and turns, steering us north toward Fort Spokane. The tranquil winding path, combined with its tight corners, sparked an instinctive response.

My mental checklist activated:

- Maintain high awareness.
- Remember, you've never actually qualified for the Isle of Man TT.
- Have fun, go ahead and scrape your pegs.

The apex is the pivotal point in a turn, hugging the arc's innermost curve. Approaching the first one felt like water surging through a turbine—a crucial moment where R69's front tire would embark on a new path. Cars usually apex at the arc's midpoint, but motorcycles, with their superior agility, can opt for an early entry or a late exit. It was up to me.

Mile by mile, we conquered the road, relishing its shape as though making love. Eventually, as the curves gave way to straighter stretches, Classy pulled over at a vantage point with a view of the Columbia River. I felt euphoric, like the blissful aftermath of great sex. Sipping water, I alternated between admiring Classy and glancing down to watch the river flow.

Motorcycle Gratitude can be overwhelming. Marta likes to quote Jaeda De Walt: "There are times I wish I were a master magician, vanishing into the folds of time, without consequence, without missing a beat."

The moment passed and my urge to press on reignited. Classy rolled away and was soon on aged, weathered pavement.

Instinctively, I steered clear of the central ridge, a repository for gravel and dripping oil. I kept R69 to the left, tracing the path where teenagers raced their parents' SUVs. Whenever a car neared, I met the driver's gaze, silently broadcasting a stern message: Stay the fuck out of my lane, NimRod!

As in life, riders must anticipate, identify, respond, and navigate past obstacles. Choices are continually made as we progress along the road, observant yet never fixated. This perpetual motion of riding, embodying control and liberty, is a stark contrast to short-span activities. Take golf, for example: its rhythm is interrupted, a pattern of brief swings interspersed with long periods of waiting. A golfer may achieve a Zen split second, but it vanishes as the swing ends and the waiting resumes. The POWER is a continuous flow.

I made a mental note to discuss with Martin the relationship between ride duration and therapeutic value.

I could smell the next corner coming up. By smoothly transitioning from one turn to the next, using the exit of each as the entry for the next, riders embody a rhythmic, sustainable motion. With religious fervor, Classy attacked and devoured each curve before slowing to adjust to the landscape. Try that on a golf course or while sitting cross-legged under a Bodhi tree.

I was 1,200 miles south of the Alaska panhandle. The two adventurers, the Coulee City Duo, would adopt the 'squeeze-as-much-in, go as far as possible, bat-out-of-hell' approach to trip plannng. I, on the other hand, had adopted a 'Start Late, Stop Early, with a Flexible Destination' philosophy. For the young men, time would serve as their guiding force, putting them off-course before their trip began.

Smarty Marty repeatedly cautioned, "Goals don't bring happiness." I was forced to ask, "So, what's the master plan, then?" What do you tell eager young riders? Depart on a whim and play it by ear? *Goals are necessary to operate efficiently, Marty.*

"Let the wheels roll. Everything else is subservient."

Marta elaborated, "Objectives are fine, but find your happiness as you move toward them."

That got me thinking: missing out on camping opportunities wasn't a big deal. Camping was a goal that would happen in its own time. Let the wheels roll toward potential camping spots—looking for happiness along the way.

I had attempted to sway the Coulee City Duo toward a route I'd taken—following the Canadian Rockies and then west along Highway 16 towards the panhandle. "Go as far as you like. Another option is the car ferry and then ride back."

However, the pair was wedded to the notion of a grand adventure. "No half measures."

"Take no prisoners."

Their get'er done attitude was admirable because their project had motorcycle merit.

I've often found myself falling into the trap of misusing time, constantly racing against the clock to meet perceived obligations that meant little or nothing to me. Many of us have misplaced notions about our criticality. The fact is, we're all ants in an anthill; the anthill thrives despite the loss of any individual contribution or where in Alaska we touch down.

Another thing Marta likes to say is, "Don't let your illusions consume you." She often winks, as if revealing a secret code.

Worrying about the future—our ambitions, successes, potential failures, aspirations, and anxieties—wastes time and blocks happiness. After my accident, I asked myself, 'Am I squandering time? Am I embracing each day as it unfolds, or am I waiting for a future reward and drowning in hesitation?'

What truly constitutes a waste of my time? Is it worthwhile to paint the trim? Or to worry about not painting the trim? To donate to the Teddy Bear run or to worry about not receiving a thankyou card? "No one's an island," Marta would say. "It's not all about you."

Huh?

Cryptic remarks like that were made for my tee shirt, the one that reads: **Tell Someone Who Cares.** I like to wear it when Dori watches the news, so I don't feel it's a complete waste of time.

Nature seemed in sync with the rhythmic pulses of the boxer engine. In my 'Commander Mike' persona, I drove down the winding road, immersed in the steady hum of the engine and the intricate patterns of the wind, in complete control. In a state of heightened awareness, I noticed every sound and sight free from judgment or attachment.

Suddenly, a noise, like a Middle East rocket barrage, jarred me from my reverie. I was momentarily disoriented. How should I react? *Had Classy thrown a rod? Seized a bearing?* My fingers instinctively squeezed the brake lever. A farm truck rounded the bend, hauling a rattling, flapping contraption. I waved. It's improper to be impolite to those who till the soil. Eager to escape the racket, I twisted the throttle, putting distance between us.

These days I prefer quiet. The Coulee City Duo had inquired, "What do you recommend for helmet speakers or earbuds? We'll need tunes for our trip." Having experimented with numerous options in the pursuit of helmet audio fidelity, I shared what had worked for me. "Now, I use audio sparingly."

Marty noted in the journal that audio can drag riders down. "Like the descent of the Titanic, it can distance you from reality, acting as an awareness diverter. Before blasting a rock anthem, consider fully engaging with your surroundings."

Really, Marty? The guy could be so melodramatic.

My take: Riding isn't about adhering to military rules. Music can relieve built-up tension and reframe negative thoughts. Blending audio with riding can be like a union of Superman and Wonder Woman. Afterward, smoke a cigarette, then turn the sound off for a while.

I doubt the Coulee City Duo embraced my suggestion of 'more silence.' They wanted a grand adventure soundtrack. The knockout punch of good tunes and wind therapy. I chose not to share this quote from the journal with them: "Our true self is ever-present and inescapable. Guitar riffs won't erase it. Instead of listening to your helmet, use riding time to connect with your inner self."

Experts say that listening to uplifting music can enhance mental focus. Therefore, Martin, music can help maintain riders' situational awareness. Loosen up buddy! Advise members to choose joyful songs like *Good Morning Sunshine* instead of *Waitin' Round to Die*.

Highway 25, a narrow, winding road, meanders through a landscape dotted with small pine trees that increasingly replace grazing lands. The friends of the deceased stag, Horace the Horrible, hang out here, so I drove cautiously, unleashing the engine's throaty defiance only in the places where open fields flanked the road.

To my left, the Columbia River continued to play peekaboo, weaving a ribbon of past adventures into my thoughts. This stretch of the river heading towards Kettle Falls is a favorite among campers, so I stopped at a small supermarket and loaded up. With a local recommendation in mind, I programmed my GPS to route me to Haag Cove Campground.

"Now it starts." I committed myself to camping before getting underway. "Like Dorothy drawn to the Emerald City." I had much to think about: meal preparation, exploring Haag Cove, and setting up camp, but still I made time to note some feedback. "Martin, isn't staying in the present moment, like trying to adhere to a stringent diet? Maybe you should moderate expectations, tone down the prescription. Like you and Marta both say, motorcycles are thinking machines. Riders aren't always going to be laser focused on the here and now."

I knew exactly what Marta's response would be. "Mike, you take things too literally."

Really, Marta? Must I be a mind reader?

Ninety minutes later, Classy arrived in Kettle Falls, its deserted main street a silent witness to the deteriorating weather. As the temperature dropped and the erratic wind gusts that had toyed with Classy gained strength, the idea of living in a tent became increasingly precarious. Then sporadic raindrops fell—small heralds of outdoor camping hell.

I stopped at a gas station to evaluate the situation. Venturing into the wilderness with only the essentials is not to be taken lightly. Looking up at the sky, it was clear to me that the light drizzle was about to escalate into a torrential downpour and gale force wind gusts were not out of the question.

Across the street, the Kettle Falls Inn looked to be a very solid refuge from the developing storm. I'd use the value of money to settle my camping conundrum; after all, every gamble has a price tag. I committed to a bottom line.

Motorcycle Camping Feedback: "There is no inclement weather, only improper gear and attire," my friend Bull of the Woods, Manny says.

The quoted room rate was $55 higher than my threshold, tilting the scale toward grinding it out at Haag Cove. I stood at a crossroads, the financial lure of continuing on to the campground versus the common sense of a motel room. I led with my doubtful look and told the owner, "I really should try out my camping gear. The weather may improve."

The man rolled his eyes. Go ahead, biker-idiot! The silence

hung heavy, like the anticipation a dirt biker feels when confronted by a daunting gap to be jumped.

Motorcycle Camping Feedback: Camping gear provides leverage. In your quest for comfort at an attractive price, bluff aggressively playing your tenting trump card.

The Kettle Falls Inn owner didn't blink. Every traveler brought a story in with them, and he'd heard them all.

I pulled my gloves on. "About twenty miles to Haag Cove, correct? Looks real nice."

The man took his time before replying, "I have a room with a fan. The air conditioner doesn't work. Twenty dollars off."

"Twenty-five." My survivalist voice countered. Or I camp!

Motorcycle Camping Feedback: Motel owners are in a war against campers. Stand your ground when their first offer falls flat.

The owner's silence left me regretting my stubbornness. I kicked myself. *Now I have to walk... over five lousy bucks?* As pleasantly as possible, I added, "Does that work?"

The owner hesitated before sliding a registration slip toward me. "Remember, no AC."

I smiled and nodded. *Any extra blankets?*

I stepped away from the negotiation battlefield, a victor in the ongoing tug-of-war between motel economics and the allure of camping.

Outside, the skies were clearing.

Motorcycle Camping Feedback: National motel chains are like motorcycles stuck in low gear. If you have a bottom line, roll your dice at a local establishment.

CHAPTER 14 –
NACHO CHEESE

I had all the ingredients needed to prepare my favorite no-cook meal. One jar of cheese sauce and a bag of multi-grain nachos. Also, pre-cut veggies and a local craft beer.

<u>Note On Riding Solo:</u> Lone riders have the liberty to dine casually, savoring home-cooked satisfying meals, rather than being dragged to the local greasy spoon.

While relishing my dinner and watching a YouTube channel about a motorcycle adventurer, a rogue drip of cheese sauce trickled down my finger. Skillfully, my tongue intercepted it before it fell on the bed.

As I watched YouTube, this question lingered: Is it possible to remain fully present while balancing the demands of filming, business management, bike maintenance, safety, and route planning? After licking the last bit of sauce from the lid of the jar, I switched the television off, brewed a cup of decaf, and opened the POWER journal.

Commanders
On the iconic path of freedom, the engine's hum merges with our heartbeats, together propelling us forward. On a motorcycle, we can

feel the motion of our lives and understand our reality. Embrace it.

As the world blurs around us, our focus remains steadfast. Suddenly, on a curve, a car swerves into our path; fear grips us and for a moment, we freeze. But our machines remain fearless. Unlike riders, motorcycles are unburdened by human traumas and so are adept at navigating danger. As commanders, we can be machine-like, never lost in the grip of fear. We picture a new line, a path around all obstacles ahead of us. Our reflexes, embedded; instinctively gauge stopping and maneuvering distances. This is how we live our lives.

Tasks abound when driving a motorcycle. Our minds must be agile and vibrant, not tired, sluggish, or weighted down by negative emotions. Before you climb on, assess your readiness. Am I prepared to take command? No one is obligated to climb on, but as Commanders, we are always in charge of our lives.

"Dead slow," Conrad answered when I asked him what a safe speed would have been the day I had my accident.

Sometimes there is no time for fear. Martin, even Commanders can be ambushed; struck by killer drones. Even at our most vigilant, our number may come up. Of course, you can also choke to death eating a cracker or the Noma Cancrum Oris virus may snuggle up in your genitals and kill you.

CHAPTER 15 - REPUBLIC

O pening my eyes, I saw droplets clinging to the roof of the tent, menacingly poised to drench me. Moving only my arm, I drew back the flap, revealing a gray, dank, unwelcoming morning.

Rubbing away the remnants of that nightmarish dream, a wave of relief swept over me. In reality, I was nestled in the cozy comfort of a Kettle Inn king-sized bed, with the first sunbeams peeking through a gap in the curtains. The temperature was ideal, without AC.

Motorcycle Camping Feedback: The experience of waking in a tent can test one's mettle.

Den has a saying, "Motorbikes belong to service departments; road trips belong to motel rooms." He's not one for camping or DIY.

In my sanctuary, I dawdled, happy to take my sweet time—it's a luxury that comes when there are no demands. I made a second cup of Kettle Falls Inn surprisingly decent coffee. The thought of waking up in a sleeping bag and needing to tear down camp made me cringe.

<u>Motorcycle Camping Feedback</u>: Often when dismantling and packing up, there's a sense of urgency to put camping in your rearview mirror.

Not quite ready, as sailors say, 'to launch an admiral,' I placed my coffee mug on the bedside table and focused on my assignment.

Do You Need a New Bike?

Most of our lives, we work to afford the things we can't enjoy because we're kept busy trying to acquire them. Eventually, you buy something on your wish list, only to discover it doesn't bring happiness, so you work to buy something better.

Money is a useful tool. With it, you can buy a motorcycle, take breaks from work to go riding, and do other things. But if you buy a newer, bigger bike, will your new thing add to the sum total of what's necessary to maintain and live a good life? Or is it a perceived value? Should you have used the time and money to actually ride the bike you had?

The allure of money is strong. It can keep you from riding while you work to get more of it. Are you in command of your choices?

Martin, you're beginning to sound like a Commie, I thought, reveling in my $25 room discount.

True Self

At work, how others perceive us determines our roles. At home, we may be a weekend warrior, parent, child, dog walker, or friend. Roles consume our lives, and we keep up the act, believing it's easier than being our true selves. We think, maybe once I overcome a certain obstacle, I'll change my ways.

We often see life clearly only after a traumatic event shakes us to our cores, possibly on our deathbed, when everything else has been stripped away. Then we reflect: what is time worth? What was real?

In this quest for clarity, motorcycles can be transformative. They force you to let go, distancing you from your perceived roles. You can see life clearly. When you step off, repeat, "Now it starts!"

◆ ◆ ◆

Classy, a vision of timeless elegance, basked in the gentle sunlight of the motel parking lot. I inched forward, captivated by the machine's allure, similar to the enchantment of human beauty, yet without the need to avert my gaze to avoid being labeled a pervert. Good morning little school girl; what price, I wondered, to call you mine?

As I eased into the comfort of the machine's sleek contours, the motel sign caught my eye, reminding me of my failure to launch. Quoting the journal, I said. "Let go of your beliefs. Flexibility is key. I'll damn well camp when I feel like it."

Being adaptable would, no doubt, ultimately lead me to a cozy experience full of camaraderie and good cheer. I imagined new friends coaxing me to join their camping happy hour. My mind painted a scene of lively guitar-led singalongs. I saw children gazing in awe at Classy while I regaled the adults with enthralling tales of my adventures. In the morning, my new friends would rouse me from my tent with freshly ground coffee while a chorus of birds sang and chipmunks frolicked. While packing, the camp ranger would drop by and reveal a nearby secret motorcycle road.

Note On Riding Solo: Fellow campers welcome lone riders and shun biker packs.

With a flick of the ignition, the engine roared, 'time to hit the road!' That's when I noticed the empty mount—my GPS was still in my travel bag. Engine off, kickstand down, step off, fumble with my gloves. Retrieve and mount SatNav. Kickstand up, gloves on, key on. The route displayed didn't look right. Sighing,

I removed my gloves to fiddle with the GPS. Frustrated, I swore as I turned the key off. Kickstand down, step off, resort to Google Maps, fix the route. Kickstand up. "Welcome back on board," I mumbled to myself. There are times riders think, 'Driving a car is so much simpler.'

Note On Riding Solo: For lone riders, forgetting something or delaying to make an adjustment is bothersome. But if you're part of a group, causing fellow riders to wait can be monumental.

Amidst these minor irritations, at the moment all systems were go, my phone beeped with a text from Smarty Marty. 'Do you golf, Mike? Earl and I are going to play nine holes at Cedar Hills. Golf is a game of stops and starts, like a bike stuck in traffic. The game offers only fleeting moments of intense focus. Unlike your day, our celebrations will be stop and go. Fun, but not a prescription.'

I know a little about golf. Golfers swing and then stand around, looking at their scores cards while waiting for others to hit their small white balls. Eventually, they take another swing —two more seconds of glory or frustration.

'There is no golf-as-therapy, Mike. Consider yourself fortunate to be riding. Bikers don't keep score and our 'swings' last for hours.'

As a casual, social-only golfer, the idea of standing around on manicured lawns or searching for lost balls never really appealed to me. I have friends who are motivated to slash a stroke or two off their games; they want to have even less to do. Does it really matter if the ball goes in the hole in four swings instead of five? Or in my case, eight instead of nine?

I replied with, "would you consider selling your R69?" but before I hit send, a follow-up arrived.

'To set expectations, I always inquire about newcomers' hobbies. My aim with golfers and the like is to shift their focus from goal-oriented activities to the art of not keeping score, encouraging them to stay present for hours instead of mere seconds. By the way, how's the camping?'

I erased my response and sent a smiley face. ☺

I was happy to be on the road rather than a member of a golf threesome, but in the back of my mind, I was keeping score: Camping 0. Motels 2.

As Classy veered west towards the town of Republic, my internal gauge read 'Fully Charged,' thanks to a good night's sleep at the Kettle Falls Inn.

I had only traveled a short distance when a juvenile grizzly sprinted out of the forest, close enough that I could see its spit flying. Muscle memory took over; my fingers instinctively clamped down on the brake lever. "Holy Mother Mary of Jesus!" I exclaimed as my right foot pressed the rear brake. Meanwhile, the bear maintained a steady trot. Unlike deer, bears have evolved; they've learned a thing or two about crossing highways without getting creamed. The grizzly soon disappeared into the underbrush on the opposite side of the narrow road.

Revving the engine, I accelerated forward. Adrenaline surging through me, energizing my senses like an extra shot of espresso. Out of nowhere, an eagle shot up from the roadside, its talons clutching a rodent. Startled, I gripped the handlebars tighter. Classy leaned into the next turn, defying gravity like the eagle that soared above.

A mile later I came up behind a slow-moving truck, its hazard lights blinking rhythmically. On its flatbed sat an enormous Caterpillar. Trailing the massive blocker, I relaxed, but boredom soon crept in and I couldn't continue playing defense.

A truth about motorcycles: motorcycles are made to lead, not follow.

Note On Riding Solo: Logic suggests that following a lead bike offers protection. Don't count on it. I was trailing Conrad when Horace the Horrible totaled my GT.

Four years had slipped away since my one and only ambulance ride. I ended up at Ferry Memorial Hospital's Emergency ward in Republic. It was a great big hullabaloo. When the dust settled, I was a different person. Devoid of energy and capability, I simply existed. I smiled to reassure friends and family, but it was a facade—inside, I was crumbling.

It's a common tale—reaching a pivotal moment, a fork in the road of life, and hearing, 'it's time to hang up your helmet. Try meditation… something that suits a low energy lifestyle. Your wild, engaged days are over.'

"Life is fleeting," Marta advised at the time, warning me not to squander it.

"Give yourself a kick in the ass," Conrad said.

"Don't be a weenie," Cam said.

Eventually, I heeded their advice, and life intensified its presence. I grew increasingly aware of how many people around me were living as though they had an inexhaustible supply of tomorrows. Rarely do people consider, 'this might be all the time I have,' or 'I may never be older than I am right now.' The present is sacrificed in the assumption there will be thousands of tomorrows. We wait for change to happen, chasing a dangling carrot.

As Classy came to a stop across from the Ferry Memorial emergency entrance, a sense of gratitude enveloped me. I nodded in silent thanks to my unseen angels of mercy, acknowledging that what happened belonged to yesterdays.

There is only here and now.

After a minute of reflection, I drove to Roaster's, a local coffee shop. Seated in a worn but comfortable patio chair, with the aroma of an Americano at hand, I opened the POWER Journal.

Tear Down Walls

Living should transcend checklists—buying that new doodad, traveling to an all-inclusive resort, rushing to live a life half known. Living should be about finding joy in the simple moments of each day. When we ride, it is clear that one mile leads to the next, each moment unfolding into another.

Don't be content to live an unremarkable life. Life should be a joyful dance, but we have a tremendous capacity to dismiss our time, reducing it to hours of getting by. It's an automatic response, but motorcycles change that dynamic the moment the wheels roll. Your eyes must be wide open—as you ride, train yourself to see the beauty in each moment.

Never dismiss time. Use your motorcycle to tear down walls. Observe your surroundings with fresh eyes, free from preconceived notions.

CHAPTER 16 – HOME OF THE KING

At the edge of their domains, where countries converge, traffic comes to a standstill. Here, freedom-loving spirits meet the process of being a nation. We wait to be declared 'benign' or 'undesirable,' hoping a digital mix-up doesn't leave us motorcycle-less and confined inside a Guantanamo Bay cage. Or is that the case anymore? Some borders have taken on a motel vibe: **Welcome! Vacancy**.

'Best be patient,' I told myself, 'and try not to look like a smuggling jackass.' In moments like this, I'm reminded, we're all tribal—bikers and nations. We're branded, modeled, and sized up; some classics, others progressives.

Classy fell silent. Helmet in hand, I braced for the inevitable interrogation, the questions that add to the tension that lingers around boundary control booths.

"How old?"

His query was ambiguous. The bike or me? "1963," I replied.

"63?" He echoed.

"Yes," I answered responsibly.

"Twenty-four years older than me."

"Ageless really."

A nod toward my license plate. "California."

"Yes."

"Bringing it home?"

Years earlier, I'd purchased what I came to call 'Movie Bike' in Berkley, California, so I was well-acquainted with the sticky Canadian importation process. "Unfortunately, no. It's not mine; it'll be heading home in a week." Unless I make Martin an offer he can't refuse. So began the paperwork review. I had lots of documents, plus a video of Martin explaining more than was necessary.

A few minutes later, the border guard asked, "Your friend uses the R69 for riding therapy… in California? Is that right?"

"Yes." I wondered if trauma and PTSD were common issues in the border protection profession.

"Interesting." His tone hinted at a deeper curiosity.

I nodded.

"Mental borders," he said, catching me off guard. "Mind if I sit on the bike for a picture?" He explained he was an off-roader, contemplating a border-to-border trip on a street bike in a year or two. "Defying regulations," he said, directing me to a blind spot.

A truth about motorcycles: motorcycles can bridge boundaries in a world defined by borders.

In the early 1900s, the Sons of Freedom, a faction of the Doukhobors, fled Russia to make their homes in the area surrounding Grand Forks, British Columbia. By the 1960s, they were branded 'outlaws' as they repeatedly gave mainstream society the finger. The Doukhobors adhere to extreme pacifism, believing that God resides in each individual rather than in structured religion. Their clash with authority, notably over compulsory military service and educational curricula, led to turmoil.

The Sons were caught in a quintessential Catch-22. In their quest for freedom, their renunciation of material possessions meant they'd turned their backs on the one tool that could have brought peace—the power of motorcycles to do good.

I made a mental note to warn Martin about the poisonous snake pit of rigid beliefs. 'They can shape destinies as surely as venom alters blood.'

On the short drive from the Danville-Carson crossing to my brother's house, I remained vigilant, keeping an eye out for protesting naked woman, a trademark of the Sons of Freedom, but I saw none. The allure of materialism is undeniable; nowadays, many Doukhobors have embraced prosperity, adopting luxury items like stylish clothing and motorbikes.

Doukhobors are stubborn and determined, traits that suit my brother Ron, a.k.a. The King of Bullheaded. He had to persevere after going down hard, first in a heavy equipment accident and later when his motorbike was side-swiped in Montevideo, Uruguay.

We rode together a few times.

Note On Riding Solo: Think of a pair of riders who share similar styles and mindsets as Tandem Solo Riders.

Given Ron's lack of interest in meal prep, I turned into the town's large supermarket for provisions. Amidst the wealth of choices, on-sale blueberries tempted my taste buds, so I grabbed two large containers and complemented them with protein bars. After checking out, I stopped at the in-store cafeteria. From my window seat, I had an excellent view of Classy in the busy parking lot. The breakfast sandwich prepared by my Doukhobor chef was the perfect accompaniment to my plump, juicy berries. It led me to a sensory contemplation.

The exact number of taste buds I possess is a mystery, but it surpasses the number my brother Ron has. We both started with around ten thousand buds. Starting between the ages of forty to fifty, humans experience taste bud decline, which eventually leads to difficulty distinguishing between sweet, sour, and bitter. Twelve years separate Ron and me. The burst of blueberry flavor confirmed that I was not yet in serious decline.

To avoid mindlessly devouring all the berries, I opened Smarty Marty's journal.

The Beginner's Mind

When I ride, the thoughts that enter my mind are rarely bothersome. They're not the mosquito-like ones you struggle to swat while trapped inside a car.

The next time you ride, try observing your thoughts as if each one is a brand-new experience. This perspective can turn the ordinary into the remarkable. Meditators call it the beginner's mind, like a child's excitement with a new toy. Don't take your thoughts too seriously or believe them to be always true. Cultivate curiosity; notice how every tree and pole beside the road is unique.

With the right mindset, riding can be the perfect environment to engage your beginner's mind.

I swiped ahead to something more concrete.

Discomfort

Depending on the bike and the rider's physical condition, prolonged sitting can become uncomfortable, even painful. Pain has many targets—knees, back, butt, or an old injury.

To alleviate this discomfort, consider a traditional meditation technique tailored for biking. Start by ensuring you maintain good posture. This means keeping your spine erect and avoiding excessive pressure on the handlebars. Periodically shift your weight to relieve any tension. As you ride, turn your attention to your breathing. Slow it down intentionally and observe the rhythm.

Next, focus on a part of your body that feels relaxed and is free of pain. After a moment, shift your focus between the area of discomfort and the relaxed part of your body. Does drawing your mind away from the pain cause the discomfort to ease?

Martin, consider adding: If that doesn't work, pull over and pop a pain pill.

The Illusion of Suffering

Motorcycle discomfort can be a learning opportunity. Use it to differentiate, to remind yourself, suffering is an illusion. Suffering is not the same as pain. Pain is a useful symptom. The Ass Problem, for example, is sending a signal—it's time for a break. Get off your bike. Move. Stretch. Deal with the pain, don't neglect it.

It's crucial to understand that pain is a physical sensation, while suffering is rooted in emotional attachments—fear, revenge, horror, jealousy, resentment, etc. Suffering is a creation of the mind, an illusion that can be dispelled. Remind yourself that you are the Commander, in control of your feelings. Unlike pain, which is a useful symptom, suffering is something that can be consciously dismissed. Don't let it escalate to a point where it becomes overwhelming.

So when you're riding and feeling discomfort, remind yourself: pain and suffering are not the same. Use the power of motorcycles to ride away from the illusion of suffering.

Following a middle-aged man out of the supermarket, I moved like a disgruntled sportbike hemmed in by traffic. Cradling protein bars and blueberries in my helmet, I observed the man ahead hunched over, burdened by a case of beer and a grocery bag. Slowly, he shuffled his feet. His downcast gaze carried an air of weariness and indifference, the unmistakable signs of a burdensome life.

Shuffler seemed like he would barely make it home,

motivated only by the prospect of the solace of alcohol. The fleeting comfort it offered would soon give way to the overwhelming weight of reality, as the bottle's contents lacked the strength to cure his apathy.

In contrast to the man's grim reality, my thoughts wandered to a potential alternative. Could the POWER alter this man's course? Rebalance his life? Might Shuffler find solace on two wheels? Switch to a different kind of intoxication? The thought intrigued me, teasing me like a distant bend in the road.

The notion of striking up a conversation occurred to me, but lacking Marta's finesse and put off by the man's body odor, I hesitated. Perhaps if I had a fancy title like 'Executive Director of Motorcyclefulness' plus a hefty NGO salary, unlimited travel budget, and some appreciation plaques, I'd have stepped forward. I imagined handing Shuffler a card saying, "We'd love to see you at group... after a shower." But that was as far as my fantasy intervention went. Unlike Smarty Marty, I'm not one of those who proselytize.

I concluded the man was likely a disenchanted Sons of Freedom Doukhobor, choosing a path other than civil disobedience. Motorcycles aren't for the faint of heart. They demand a resolute spirit and Shuffler had lost his.

The boxer engine came to life and my beginner's mind switched on.

As midafternoon settled in, friends arrived with wine, beer, and snacks, setting the stage for happy hour. Ron mentioned some of his guests had roots that go back to Russian Doukhobor communities. "Good people," he declared, nodding to reinforce his approval.

"Blueberries, anyone?" I offered my new acquaintances.

We relaxed on Ron's large front porch, trading motorcycle

anecdotes.

"Early bikes couldn't go over forty miles an hour."

"Ever fallen off a bike wearing only shorts? Hurts like hell, let me tell you."

"I say motorcycles need two more wheels."

"Here, dirt riding is king."

"It's one way to meet your maker."

"I've always fantasized about cruising free and easy like Easy Rider. Maybe one day, I will."

As we swapped stories and I listened to dreams of adventures yet to unfold, this thought occurred to me: lone riders understand how far they can stretch their independence bungee cords before seeking companionship, be it at a rest stop, parking lot, gas station, or visiting a brother.

Note On Riding Solo: The solitude of a journey often magnifies the joy found in shared moments.

The conversation naturally flowed from the porch to the carport, where we gathered for an up-close look at the R69S. "Highly reliable tourer, extremely collectible. Less than 1,200 produced. Set you back two or three new bikes to buy one in decent shape today. Been an unforgettable experience… the ride here."

"Kickstart?"

"Electric," I responded with a shrug. "May have been retrofitted."

"Engine sticks out."

"Boxer… opposed cylinders."

"Horsepower?"

"594cc. Half the size of modern highway bikes, but it's no slouch."

As my new friends snapped pictures, I wondered whether any motorcycle in history could rival the R69. Harley Knuckheads?

The Honda 90? Early Indians or Triumphs? Old Royal Enfields or Nortons? Among the many names that evoke humanity's potential for greatness, it was Classy who held court in Ron's driveway on that day.

In the midst of admiring the R69, I remembered a question Marta often posed: 'does your bike have a personality?' It always sparked contemplation as one recalled the machines they'd ridden. Until Conrad called horseshit. "They're design decisions with manufacturing compromises."

Marta, however, insists "Guzzi certainly is a character."

Classy exudes confidence and always makes a good first impression. In the world of motorcycles, each has its own allure. Some beckon with a friendly invitation, while others snicker. "Keep your distance; I'm temperamental and a bit of a show-off."

"There's an uncanny parallel," Marta suggests. "Between motorcycles and riders. Getting the match right is critical."

On the porch, observing each person, I matched each guest with a bike that suited their personality.

Note On Riding Solo: Those who journey alone don't always seek solitude.

As the evening progressed, our topics wandered, landing curiously on the rising prices of supermarket roasted chickens. "You have to be a man of means to buy a chicken these days."

Switching from bikes to chickens didn't faze Ron. His resilience, born from enduring a horrendous accident when he was a young man (described in *Scraping Pegs, The Truth About Motorcycles*), forced him to be tenacious. The King of Bullheaded, I call him.

Restoring health can be a demoralizing task, given the lack of a guarantee. Picture the frustration of bringing your bike to Service, only to be told they can't provide an expected completion date or assure you their efforts will be successful. If the finish line is distant, like Ron's was, you must be bullheaded to succeed.

The last word on supermarket roasted chickens: "Sometimes they're discounted. Try going late on Sundays." Practical wisdom.

As I listened to the conversations flow across the porch, I felt a sense of gratitude, both for my journey and for the company of strangers. I took a moment to send a photo to Tony's gang with the caption, 'Relaxing at my brother's. No camping tonight. Excited about pitching my tent tomorrow.' ☺

Returning with snack bowls in hand, I discovered the group deeply engrossed in a discussion about their friend Lavel's troubles. The atmosphere, once lighthearted, was woven with concern. Arnie weighed in somberly, "He's in a world of hurt." After thirty-one years of marriage, Lavel faced a shocking betrayal: his wife had drained their bank account and got the hell out of Grand Forks.

Amidst the quiet murmurs, Deri Latimer offered her perspective, attributing Lavel's escalating troubles to self-inflicted wounds. Brimming with optimism, she stopped by her friend's place on the way to Ron's. "Dropped off the book," she said. "*The Pathway to Happiness*." She believed that if Lavel could overcome self-pity and apply himself, the wisdom in the book would 'right his ship.'

The friends nodded—at least it was something. It seemed a more constructive option than simply taking their buddy for drinks and getting him hammered.

"I told Lavel to focus on the worst-case scenario for the next couple of days," Deri said. "Envision the most daunting, bleakest outcomes. This approach will soften the blow of his current situation, priming him for the solutions offered in the book."

Really Deri? Instead of *The Pathway to Happiness*, why not introduce your friend to Shuffler? It'd be a distraction and Shuffler would gain a drinking buddy.

"May backfire," Arnie replied, his skepticism as entrenched as tire tracks in wet earth. "The path to happiness ain't in a book."

Unfazed by Arnie's skepticism, Deri countered, insisting the wisdom to be found in *The Pathway to Happiness* was exactly what Latimer required.

I thought about mentioning the POWER Journal, but Deri seemed adamant and Ron's porch wasn't the place for Gearhead Gandhi.

That evening, as I flipped through the King of Bullheaded's untouched copy of *The Pathway to Happiness*, a passage caught my eye: "Happiness is the ability to feel free; to be your authentic self, regardless of how others react. It's believing that everything will be okay because you've cultivated a state of emotional well-being. You're not trapped by the past and its effects on you. What your future holds is your choice."

That's pretty much how I feel when I'm riding.

I was pleased with my answer until a statement on the following page cast doubt on my way of thinking. "True happiness comes from inside you; it is not derived from material possessions."

Really, Pathways author? The fact is, money buys the freedom to ride, and that leads to true happiness. I called horseshit on omitting material possessions, especially ones with two wheels.

"There isn't a formula because happiness is up to you," the author discloses to readers after they've wasted hours plowing through most of the book. *Copout alert! Why not admit you don't have an answer on page one?* Here's my advice: move to San Jose and join Smarty Marty's community.

As nightfall blanketed Grand Forks, the moon shed its gentle glow over Ron's large yard. I could have pitched my tent and spent a calm night outside. But when provided the option of a tent or the comforts of a guest room, adults always choose the guest room.

I turned to what had become a welcome companion, the POWER Journal.

Your Journey

In life, as in riding, we're perpetually moving forward. A glance in the rearview mirror reminds us of where we've been, but our journeys are firmly rooted in what lies ahead. We must focus on the present and the road ahead.

Riding is a journey like life condensed in time.

Revving Up Your Mind

After forty, it's common for human brains to change gradually, often experiencing a decrease in volume and weight—about 5% per decade. This can involve a reduction in nerve cells and a contraction of gray matter, potentially impacting our cognition. Despite these natural changes, there is a silver lining. Engaging in mentally stimulating activities can help decelerate or even counteract this decline. Studies have shown that activities requiring active engagement and coordination can serve as high-intensity brain exercises. The gold standard of cognitive stimulation—motorcycles. Use yours to nourish your brain and feed your well-being.

Unleashing Fluid Thought

Rigid mindsets can trap us in a spiral of negativity, much like being stuck in a mental labyrinth. As you embark on your journey, allow your thoughts to flow freely, exploring the landscapes of possibilities. As it is traveling on two wheels, where the wind acts as a lubricant, our thoughts need to flow freely, steering us towards new horizons.

Ride to maintain a fluid, active mind that doesn't bog down in mental stagnation. Don't allow yourself to stall out. The journey of a thousand miles begins with a single rotation. Now it starts!

Which Tool?

Every self-help pitch boils down to the same set of points. Adopt positive beliefs. Learn from past mistakes. Banish negative thoughts. Be mindful. Accept yourself and so on. All are excellent suggestions; however, intangibles fail to make a lasting impact. That's why people are forever moving on to the next pitch.

Noticeably absent from mainstream advice is 'ride a motorcycle'. Test all the recommendations and then go for a ride. Ask yourself: which wellness tool cleared my mental clutter the best?

Heeding the well-known advice of experts about screen time, I powered down my phone. I'm a lousy sleeper, a trait common in my family. We've tried all the self-help remedies without success.

I always sleep well after a motorcycle ride.

CHAPTER 17 - STOP
OF INTEREST

In the Pacific Ocean, Mother Nature was orchestrating a meteorological Black Swan. "So, which will it be? South, west, or stay put?" Ron asked.

I faced a choice of diverging paths, each with uncertain outcomes. Choosing the wrong way home could lead to an open-air battle with the elements, spiraling into a case of Motorcycle Misery.

I'm no stranger to shitty weather—plummeting temperatures and that insidious moisture that creeps into openings and seeps beneath rain gear. Fingers go numb, but you twist the throttle, hoping to reach shelter before you succumb. You're like a cowboy in an old western movie, slumped over the saddle, dependent on your trusty steed to reach the O.K. Corral. 'Next time I'll take the stagecoach,' the cowboy vows. But then it clears up, and he gallops into the sunset.

A truth about motorcycles: If bikers were averse to risk, including bad weather, they wouldn't be bikers in the first place.

"Think classics have bad weather immunity?" I asked.

A truth about motorcycles: Mother Nature can be a cunt . It's one reason there are cars.

◆ ◆ ◆

On a Friday morning, geared up for whatever the warm front lingering in the Pacific Ocean decided to do, I resumed my journey traveling westward rather than south and over to the ferry at Port Angeles, Washington. Before confronting Vancouver's urban sprawl, Highway 3 would reveal high mountain passes, meandering rivers, serene lakes, towering rock cliffs, dense forests, quaint towns, and vast grasslands. Everything R69s were designed for would grace Classy's presence.

Ron's parting words were cautious: "Your bike's getting old, Mike. Take it easy." I didn't explain Classy's remarkable defiance of aging. This Beemer, over half a century old, would outlast the typical lifespan of a human body. Unlike human bones that weaken from nutrient loss, metal frames like Classy's can be stripped, welded, sandblasted, re-coated, and restored to their original glory. In contrast, our skeletons shrink as we age, the disks between vertebrae losing fluid and thinning.

Old motorcycles face their own aging challenges—metal fatigue, dried-out gaskets, and electrical faults—similar to how human bodies lose flexibility, weaken, and suffer from pain and stiffness. The difference is that restoring a motorcycle doesn't require an act of God; meticulous care will suffice. Classy, theoretically, could stay on the road forever.

Lost in thoughts about motorcycle longevity versus human lifespans and its implications for Smarty's project, Ron's warning brought me back: "And watch for deer."

"No problemo," I replied.

"Problema," he corrected me with a wry smile.

I shrugged it off—*whatever, Ron. In the world of motorcycle lingo, it's 'problemo.'*

An hour outside Grand Forks, I caught sight of a weathered sign that read **Point of Interest.** *What curiosity did the multi-disciplinary government body and their consultants deem worthy?* I didn't have high hopes. Neither did the cagers who, intent on reaching their destinations, ignored the attraction, resulting in an unintended consequence. If you have to pee, Points of Interest are a godsend.

I turned into a small gravel parking area. A few cars sped by.

I thought, 'I'm here; may as well find out what prompted the sign.' My attention shifted to a protected area, a breeding ground for secretive grasshopper sparrows. I tipped my helmet to the little birds, then took a leak, checking to ensure no birds had strayed into the spray area. Points of Interest never disappoint, as long as you have to pee.

'Somewhat Interesting Relief Stop' ahead would be a better sign; the words 'For Bikers' being implied.

Leaning against Classy with my water bottle in hand, a Zen saying I'd read in the journal came to mind: "With the ideal comes the actual," meaning the spiritual and the material are interconnected and harmonious. It's true. I'd pulled in to handle a basic necessity but felt a connection with everything around me. Nothing was lacking. Everything was as it should be. Classy. The sparrows. My dry bag. The sign. This place. The road. The vegetation I watered. Baby sparrows being stalked by snakes in the grass.

Then, abruptly, the peaceful bubble of my thoughts burst with the jarring rumble of a motorcycle speeding by. I yelled after the thundering machine, "Don't you need to pee?" *Don't you want to swap road stories? Perhaps debate how loud is too loud?*

Something felt off. I watched as the landscape swallowed the lone rider.

Note On Riding Solo: "We are all alone, born alone, die alone, and we shall all someday look back on our lives and see that, in spite of our company, we were alone the whole way. I do not say lonely —at least, not all the time—but essentially, and finally, alone. This is what makes your self-respect so important, and I don't see how you can respect yourself if you must look in the hearts and minds of others for your happiness." - Hunter S. Thompson, The Proud Highway.

Loud pipe rider had zoomed by without waving. I wondered, did Classy's grandeur intimidate? Had our bikes been more alike, might he have stopped?

Whatever, buddy. Your company isn't necessary for my happiness. I walked over and focused my attention on the 'Mating Rituals of the Grasshopper Sparrow.' It was quite interesting.

◆ ◆ ◆

As Classy approached a stretch of sweepers, I felt like a racer at the starting line—everything was possible. Then the tires caressed the coal-black curves, carving perfect arcs with the grace and precision of an Olympic speed skater.

Eventually, as happens with roads, the excitement gave way to Steady Eddie calm. Soon there was a slow-moving truck, a double white line, and a dip in the road. I bided my time, eager to cease being a follower. The once adventurous hum of Classy's engine settled into a dull drone; my moments of exuberance had slipped into tedium.

I recalled a journal entry that posed this question: 'What is boredom?' The answer: 'Boredom is simply your mind being lazy.'

After a few minutes, my impatience faded away, replaced by the predictability of routine. The road now cradled me in its familiar rhythm. Marta's words echoed in my mind. "Sometimes you need to slow down to speed up."

Really, Marta? Maybe if you're on a Guzzi.

With a surge, I overtook the lumbering truck. As Classy cast off the cloak of impatience, a rebellious spirit grew within me, prompting a yell of defiance.

A truth about motorcycles: Scream all you want. No one will suspect you're mad or out of control.

Having reclaimed the road, I eased back to eleven over the posted limit.

In the tourist town of Osoyoos, failing to spot a local coffee shop, I settled for the familiar comfort of the golden arches.

Of course, the POWER journal accompanied my coffee.

Don't Look Elsewhere

St. Francis of Assisi, renowned for his profound spiritual insights, once said, 'What we are looking for is already within us.' This message, though seemingly simple, carries a deep truth that resonates beyond its context. As we crest a hill or come out of a bend, a new horizon greets us. On the road, the world constantly changes, yet we feel ourselves becoming who we really are. It can happen because all the peace, wisdom, and joy in the universe are already within us. To discover it, we must sweep away our mental clutter. In these moments, a voice whispers, 'You are the embodiment of truth, from your boots to your helmet. What else is there to discover?'

In a world brimming with endless distractions, riding can be a journey of revelation. It reminds us that what we seek—truth, understanding, peace—is not scattered in the external world, but lies nestled within the depths of our being. As you ride, let the words of St. Francis resonate within you, reminding you that the journey is within.

Ride Away

Riding strips away our self-imposed limitations and illusions. Such is the power of motorcycles—they cannot only transport us across landscapes but reveal our inner diamonds. As you ride, let each mile take you further away from your preconceived notions and closer to the essence of who you are. Leave behind the familiar and welcome who you are.

I pushed the kickstand up and set off, unaware of what I might find ahead. One moment I was planted on the ground, the next I was balancing above it, elevated both physically and mentally.

I was a person happy to be where I was. While riding, gratitude doesn't clamor for our attention. Often taken for granted, it can remain unnoticed for many miles, shunning the spotlight. Sports teams conduct pep talks before competitions. Golfers concentrate on practice swings. Religions have elaborate commencement rituals. With motorcycling, just push the kickstand up and know 'what I am looking for is within me.'

The wheels are round and they roll.

Fruit stands dot the highway through the orchard town of Keremeos. Arriving at the height of cherry season, I found that even in this bountiful land, you had to be a person of means to afford cherries. Inclined to be extravagant, I purchased a small basket, reasoning that since I'd be camping , I could splurge on expensive fruit.

Sitting at a wooden picnic table, I enjoyed the succulent sweetness of the cherries, savoring each one before discreetly spitting out the pit. Behind me, rows of trees stood like silent sentinels, pleased to witness their seed being returned to the earth. To distract myself from mindless eating, I swiped to open the journal.

Control

Events happen around us over which we have no control. It puzzles us. What is within my power to control? How can I influence my circumstances? What is going on?

You can't control the actions of the world around you. True dominance lies within—over our reactions, our mindset, and our choices. Amid unpredictable events, it's crucial to accept that things will happen to you and you must prepare yourself. While you can't prevent a reckless driver from swerving into your lane or unexpected debris from obstructing your path, you can improve your readiness and control how you respond. External forces are beyond your domain; the only thing you have control over is yourself.

Your identity is shaped not by what happens to you, but by how you respond. Focus on what you have the power to change—yourself.

As I considered my over indulgence—the fact that I had no control over the cost of cherries, but could have prevented myself from purchasing—the roar of an approaching army of bikes snapped me back to the present. Everyone at the fruit stand turned their attention to the road. I spit out a pit and thought, one shouldn't jump to conclusions. For all I knew, the riders may have been florists, lawyers, orderlies and other assorted weekend warriors on a cherry run.

The platoon slowed, possibly to investigate Classy, but then carried on. No doubt some hoped to pull in, but if you're not the lead bike, in a group, you're obliged to follow.

<u>Note On Riding Solo</u>: Lone riders always lead.

I counted fourteen bikes. I wished they'd stopped. "Isn't it dangerous riding in a group?" I'd ask, eager to hear their defense. They may have shot me their hard-ass, get-lost glare. More likely, they'd tell me I was full of horseshit, to ride alone. "We're seen! No one notices you on your own."

Those words would bring the gavel down, even so, there'd be more. "And we're heard."

I'd nod. *Whatever. That hardly justifies riding with a bunch of jackasses.*

<u>Note On Riding Solo</u>: Solo riders don't pay attention to the saying, 'there is safety in numbers.'

CHAPTER 18 - A GOOD SPOT

B romley Rock Provincial Campsite is nestled in a picturesque valley, where a sandy beach converges with a river pool, across from a towering bluff. I arrived at 3 p.m., leaving ample time for a rusty outdoorsman to set up camp. As Classy's sound filled the tranquility with a reassuring strength, I thought, 'Martin, your strategy of blending motorcycling with camping has merit.'

As I drove down the narrow road, I half-expected to be greeted by a **Welcome To Your Spot** sign, the campsite's version of a motel's **Vacancy**. Instead, Bromley Rock confronted me with stark red 'stay-the-hell-out of this reserved spot,' markers. Just two out of the eighteen sites were not occupied. I circled back to the visitor board to check the status of the unreserved sites. A printout in minuscule font detailed the current status. Of the two spots that weren't reserved, one was already occupied, leaving only the least desirable patch of dirt and gravel available.

Motorcycle Camping Feedback: Parking a vintage motorcycle next to an outhouse reeking of cager cherry diarrhea is unthinkable.

Motorcycle Camping Feedback: Camping authorities set aside

sites for the handicapped, all manner of RVs, walk-ins, nonbinaries, and large groups, but there is a glaring omission; the state gives two-wheel, small tent, low-impact campers the finger. Is it any wonder we're rebels?

The situation at Bromley Rock was untenable. Refusing to let this setback dampen my enthusiasm, I consulted Google Maps for an alternative. It revealed a municipal campground close to the town of Princeton. City-owned campgrounds, designed to bolster local economies, present an ideal choice for soft-core campers. Their proximity to town offers a seamless blend of urban convenience and wilderness adventure, often at below-market rates.

In my mind, Classy executed a long wheelie out of Bromley Rock.

Back on the highway, as the R69S picked up speed, two identical crotchrockets overtook me. Despite the apparent contradiction, Cam has always maintained that superbikes are the safest vehicles on the road due to their unparalleled agility, which allows them to avoid potential hazards.

"Sure Cam," I'd agree skeptically.

Conrad might add: "And get into trouble faster and die sooner."

Cam concedes that if riders' skills don't match the capabilities of their hyper-performing bikes, the machines are potential death traps.

"The road's a metaphor for life's exuberance," Marta would say. "Crotchrockets mirror the folly and courage of youth... then you buy a Guzzi."

Seeing both brake lights on at the first curve's apex, I knew Classy had a chance to catch the racers, as long as they remained on the road. *They don't know corners like we do, Classy.* They don't see through the entry, the apex, and the exit with an instinct to remain the master, fully in control. With an intense concentration, I charged ahead with a single-minded purpose. Devour the corner and chase them down.

Within two more bends, I was nearly upon them. The sports bikes, trying to widen the gap, accelerated on the short straight sections before braking, going into the curves.

There's a saying: 'speed variance kills,' implying 'adapt to the flow,' even if it means exceeding the speed limit. So I played it safe and kept pace with the crotchrockets.

Another saying warns: 'speed thrills before it kills.' My body was feeding on adrenaline. Picture this: an old classic mid-sized bike overtaking Born To Be Wild SQUIBs on rockets. Before dropping back, I savored the moment. I remembered the danger of being pushed when I was full of piss and vinegar. When there was more vanity and testosterone than common sense.

A POWER journal entry prompted me to reflect. "Our brains guide and direct our machines. They're wondrous things, but our three-pound pieces of meat need to be aged. Exposed, they're pulsating, glistening marvels, absorbing stimuli, crafting thoughts. Add a drop of adrenaline and they feel invincible. If you're in that category, pull rank on your brain and tell it to grow up. Never allow yourself to be pushed beyond your comfort zone. "

My mature brain agreed. I didn't want to witness crotchrockets wrapped around trees with brains smeared over bark, and be forced to stop to assist what remained of two bikers-in-distress. Talk about a moment you don't want to be in.

Classy glided to a perfect rolling stop beside the Princeton Municipal Campground's office entrance, my left foot touching down on an imaginary bullseye. Proud of my performance, I scanned the area—surely the couple walking their dog witnessed my skillful maneuver? I stepped off nonchalantly, as if my middle name was Graceful. The dog walkers glanced toward Classy and nodded—hi there, free spirited, skilled rider.

As I took in the sun-drenched scene of well-appointed facilities and natural beauty, I felt I'd truly arrived. This was it, without a doubt. I took a photo of the entrance sign and had a caption in mind—the motorcycle camper has landed!

The moment I entered the office, a gentleman with a radiant smile greeted me. "Certainly. We have a spot for you," he assured me.

With a sense of harmonious alignment, I formed a happy-go-lucky smile. *Perhaps I'll invite the camp manager to drop by later, after I've picked up a few cans of beer.*

The conversation shifted as the manager inquired about my preference. "Would you prefer a river view or closer to the washrooms? Some like a short walk," he said. "Not an issue for you, I'd wager." Before I could answer, he added, "The ones along the river are a bit smaller."

"Just me and my tiny tent. River view, please." The manager began the process and I asked, "How much for my little tent?"

"Sixty-six bucks. Seventy-five with taxes."

The price bounced me out of my shorts like an unseen pothole. "Bromley Rock was only twenty-eight."

The man laughed. "Haven't camped for a while, hey? Those days are long gone, my friend."

"Motorcycles with tiny tents are charged the same price as forty foot RVs?"

"Yup. Unless they want hookups. Everyone has access to the indoor washrooms and showers."

Whatever, buddy. I'll pee behind a tree and washup in the river.

While the price tag was within my means, the value proposition stunk. Sleeping in the countryside, on public ground, should cost little more than nothing. After all, urban sidewalk and city park campers aren't charged a cent and are provided with loads of free stuff.

I did the math: for an extra few dollars, a budget motel

would provide a bed, washroom, AC, Wi-Fi, TV, coffee, and snake protection.

<u>Motorcycle Camping Feedback</u>: For many, camping is a budget stretcher, enabling longer trips. But unless you bushwhack or pitch your tent in a hospitable biker's backyard, the savings can be underwhelming.

The manager and I engaged in a discussion about the unfairness of the campground's pricing policy toward motorcycles and single-person tents. I casually dropped the word "discrimination," thinking it might prompt the town's Director of Equality and Fairness to intervene. Instead, after reflecting on the economic nuances of campground operations, the manager replied, "Life's like that. Does it matter given you can afford to cruise around on your expensive motorcycle?"

I shrugged. *Whatever, jackass.* Freedom's value extends beyond money to the decisions that guide our lives, so, on principle, I gave the price of nature the biker salute and buggered off.

I made a point of mentioning that I'd stayed a year earlier when the new owners were beginning renovations. "One of your first customers, I expect. This time, I'm on a camping trip... carrying a tent." I left the unspoken implication hanging in the air, 'and I'm not afraid to use it.'

The Asian motel owner, her eyes twinkling with a hint of mischief, then offered a modest repeat customer discount, welcoming me back like an old friend. "Only for returning motorcyclists," the owner declared with a grin, justifying the discount. "You guys use less parking space."

"Deal," I proclaimed, delighted with our interaction. With a discount in play, the option of overpaying to sleep on public ground had no appeal.

<u>Motorcycle Camping Feedback</u>: It's good to have a camping bottom line.

I'd put the question to Marta before I left. "How much should I aim to save in exchange for sleeping on the ground?"

"Disregard the numbers. It's not about the money."

Really, Marta? If it's not about the numbers, what is it about? After taking in miles of the great outdoors, there's nothing glamourous about sleeping with Mother Nature.

As I lay sprawled on the motel bed, my gaze naturally went to the ceiling. Clearly, the owners had put significant effort into updating the room, yet they had overlooked one of its key elements. I suppose ceilings are like the underside of motorcycles.

Apart from the ceiling, the motel was presentable and well-equipped with everything necessary. I had half a mind to return and present a list of the municipal campground's deficiencies when compared to my competitively priced private room. But the thought of being cited in the monthly report as an example of 'retaining tourist business' made it unappealing. So I stared at the ceiling for a while before sitting up and reading the journal.

Happiness

Everyone has a feeling they call happiness. The idea of happiness forms like a seed in our minds, and then we undertake a mission to satisfy the notion. But happiness is not something we can check off a list.

Happiness is a state of heightened awareness, a harmonious blend of contentment, peace, and joy. Riding is also a state of heightened awareness that can lead to a harmonious blend of contentment, peace, and joy. Ride and find not only the path to happiness, but the realization that it has always been within you.

Turning the page, the journal posed the question: What is the point of waiting?

Why Wait?

What exactly are we waiting for? Is someone going to hand us everything we've ever wanted?

As you ride, realize, nothing is as precious as who you are now.

Throughout our life's journey, we frequently encounter moments of waiting, desperately holding onto the hope of gaining something in the future. But ride and our veils of distortion fade away. So, I ask again, what are we waiting for? Remember, the journey is now, and we have everything needed.

The stubborn room lock brought to mind the gas cap on one of my ex-motorcycles. Both uncooperative and finicky, demanding my undivided attention. As I worked on opening the door, my phone broke the silence with a message from Cam.

Inspired by my trip, my friend was considering a Rocky Mountains adventure camping trip. He wanted to know if I was interested? *Are you kidding me?* The Rockies are hardcore, not for those who wrestle with locks.

Cam's personality is a study in contrasts: often rash and over the top, yet he's also capable of deep introspection and total absorption. A musician, he talks about reaching a place where only sound exists. "The music that once lay on the page is now within me," he says. "Riding is the same experience. It's all music, or all ride."

Escape doesn't come easily to me. I am a purposeful person. Letting go is a project; I cling to my preferences, such as beds, lockable rooms, and toilets that flush.

'What a fantastic idea,' I typed. 'Camping in the Rockies. But by the time I get home, I'll have had my fill of the great outdoors. Manny, the mountaineer is the guy you want.'

Motorcycle Camping Feedback: Balance is key in camping; not everyone wants to climb Mount Everest.

'Maybe I'll go solo, like you,' Cam replied.

I wrote back: 'Ask Manny... or maybe Dolores. She's been wanting to try motorcycle camping.'

As Legs, unburdened, clad only in shorts and sandals, walked me towards the town center, I left all doubts behind. My confidence surged with each step. If Cam can take on the Rockies, I can conquer the Cascades. Manning Provincial Park, tomorrow's destination, waited with its vast expanse of wilderness opportunities: four drive-in campsites, eleven walk-in sites, and countless opportunities to go rogue and camp anywhere.

Unlike the towering Rockies, Manning Park was approachable, like the smooth action of a high-quality lock. Tomorrow, I'd enter and embrace its playground, a sensible sanctuary where I'd fulfill my destiny of being a roving crusading therapeutic riding contributor.

Suddenly, my senses were overcome by an enticing smell

coming from a country barbeque restaurant. Legs made a hard right.

Motorcycle Camping Feedback: Before surrendering to the wilderness, feed your body.

CHAPTER 19 -
FULL FLUSH

At gas station restrooms, neglect and demonstrations of poor technique are the norm. Campgrounds are even worse—cager shit is sometimes smeared on walls and urine puddles on floors. Public washrooms put me off of the 'here and now.' It's one reason travelers rent motel rooms—to enjoy benign toilet experiences.

But a sign placed at eye level above my motel toilet implored, **"Please Flush Fully."** Did they somehow recognize that I was a half-hearted public toilet handle tapper? To compensate, I often execute the equivalent of double clutching: flush, wait, and flush again using my boot.

Flushing private toilets, like driving on the proper side of the road, is a societal norm—so why was there a sign above my toilet? It invited disrespect. Signs often feel like weapons of mass authority, yelling, 'Obey! Don't be a thinker, be a follower!' They clash with motorcycle cultural norms. **Please Flush Fully** disrespected my toilet rental expectations, which pissed me off.

When I voice my sign aggravation, Marta tells me, "Signs are inert, Mike. It's your brain that's on fire."

Really, Marta? I trust my brain and let it think for itself. My brain doesn't need dumb signs bossing it around.

Stepping away from the toilet, I wondered: Are vacationers the worst culprits? *It's my time, and I refuse to waste it dealing with substandard plumbing.* Or is it a problem with execution, like eliminating the final air bubble when bleeding brake lines?

Had the sign instructed **User Must Flush Fully,** I'd definitely have given it the biker salute. The word **'please'** made the sign tolerable. Considering the motel owners had extended a repeat customer discount, I not only flushed, I stood by and monitored the operation. I'm not unreasonable.

<u>Note On Riding Solo</u>: Riders, especially lone riders, often treat signs as suggestions.

Had I been sharing with a riding buddy, it'd be an automatic full flush, including a do-over if required. No one wants to leave their floaties on display.

<u>Note On Riding Solo</u>: Lone riders don't have to deal with peer pressure.

<u>Motorcycle Camping Feedback</u>: The idyllic vision of camping in nature is often shattered by the mere thought of the outhouse visit.

Although I have a strong dislike for certain signs, I acknowledge that many of them serve a practical function. Mainly I've grown impatient with misleading signs like **'Slow to 45.'** **'Cagers Slow to 45'** would be acceptable. Also pointless signs like **'No Littering.'** **'Litterers Will Be Shot,'** would be acceptable. What really bugs me is the realization that the people-in-charge-of-putting-things-on-signs treat their audience as if we're idiots. I'm amazed the UN hasn't struck a sign initiative. **'No Bombing Here.'** **'Use Correct Pronouns.'** That sort of thing. '**No Fossil Fuels, Unless Flying On UN Business**.'

I shouldn't let a dumb sign twist my awareness like a bent

rim. I'll talk to Smarty Marty about beefing up the journal, adding a note about dealing with triggers. Mind you, on-motorcycle, dumb signs are inconsequential.

Reflecting on my changing attitudes, I realized in many respects, I'm more selfish now than I was a decade ago. I'm definitely less tolerant of intrusions. Back then, I'd willingly follow suggestions without giving them a second thought. I went along, contributing to the greater good. Friends noticed I had a glow about me. Mike is so considerate... for a curmudgeon. Now I'm less tolerant and no longer glow. Fix the damn plumbing instead of telling me how to flush!

I think it's normal to start off thick-skinned and become thin-skinned. Smarty should look into this. It may explain why wind therapy becomes more effective with age—its ability to penetrate improves.

For me, at this time in my thin-skinned life, solitude on two wheels is the ultimate diversion; I'm better at absorbing its values. When I was younger, my bikes were three parts adrenaline, two parts whoop-d-doing, and one part trash removal.

Now it doesn't take many miles for me to fully flush.

CHAPTER 20 -
BELL CURVE

As I surveyed Manning Provincial Park for the ideal camping spot, I behaved like a stereotypical tourist, oohing and aahing ad nauseam. No wonder so many explorers were drawn to the wilderness Before Motorcycle. I drove through spectacular scenery, free from modern disruptions, save for the occasional highway distraction.

It was past eleven o'clock, and the campgrounds were buzzing with life, stakes were being pulled out and sites vacated. Tall trees shaded the first main campground, leaving little sunlight, so I drove on. Who wants to sit in the gloom, alone, waiting for first light so you can bugger off? At the second location, hordes of campers with towels around their necks were shuffling toward the washroom. It put me off; the visit is traumatic enough without waiting in a queue forced to size up the shit ahead of you.

Motorcycle Camping Feedback: Camping makes for busy days. Rising early from your tent, you pack up, strike camp, and load gear onto your bike. Before leaving, you check your route, scouting for potential stops. Then you hit the road praying for a recently cleaned indoor public washroom. Throughout the day, you remain vigilant, constantly on the lookout for camping signs and frequently pulling over to check Google Maps. As evening approaches, panic strikes—the fear of being a homeless lone camper sets in. After encountering a 'Closed' sign and enduring a longer-than-expected ride, you finally find a spot next to a dump site at the far end of South Shit Creek Road. You unpack, set up camp, and then either cook or climb back on your bike to head to the gas station store. Because you're alone, and have nothing to do, so you go to bed at eight-thirty. In the morning, you have difficulty rounding up your clothes and then struggle to pull your riding pants up while lying on your back. When you crawl out of your tent, you're irritated by this thought: if I'd stayed at a motel, I'd be relaxing with a cup of coffee. Everything you unpacked and set up hours ago must be reversed. At last ready to depart, you find the park gate still locked, with no contact number in sight. A morning walker tells you, "they run on camper time."

Martin, if you decide to tag camping onto therapy rides, consider mitigation. Use The Long Way Down model. They had a support truck equipped with a cook, mechanic, first aid professional, generator, and other necessities. Think like a motorcycle tour operator. You don't want inexperienced tenters freaking out because their stakes won't hold or their phones can't be charged.

Approaching the Manning Park exit, I realized I'd witnessed a perfect example of the bell curve in action. Of the twenty opportunities, only four campgrounds were in the running— two at the entry approaching the mountains, and two on downhill slopes before the exit. The rest were for those who wanted to pretend they were at the Mount Everest Base Camp. I contemplated going back to the last campground, but I have a strong aversion to backtracking.

Shortly after exiting Manning Park, Classy pulled into the Hope

Slide viewing area. In 1965, a massive landslide occurred when 47 million cubic meters of a Cascade Mountain slope gave way. The incident tragically took four lives, serving as a somber reminder of how unpredictable nature can be.

Given the danger of being crushed and smothered by a mountain, I abandoned the idea of returning to Manning Park. As I set my sights on my next camping target, my attention shifted to a young man adjusting the chain slack on his fixer bike. Worn sprocket? Stretched chain? The fixer, worn down by years of neglect, seemed to groan, 'everything about me is fucked-up.' In contrast, the R69 represented the pinnacle of what is possible.

The stranger, looking disheartened as he crouched by the rear wheel, kept his eyes fix on Classy. No amount of effort would elevate his bike to Classy's level. I've been there, fooling myself that spit, polish, and adjustments would turn my machine into a beauty.

As a rider of modest means, I started out owning It'll Do Bikes with past due service reminders. I'm still not one of those who owns a stable of bikes, but years ago, I shifted my priorities, moving 'motorcycle' close to the top of my 'what to spend money on' list.

The young man had me pegged as a member of the fat cat gearhead tribe. I could have parked Classy further away to avoid the comparison, but I'd earned the right to park wherever the hell I wanted. *There's nothing wrong with being on your knees, kid. I paid my dues. Now it's my turn to gloat.*

Lord knows I've spent time on my knees. Even now, owning an expensive bike doesn't grant immunity form breakdowns. When it happens, fat cats of real means call their gold star rescue services. Riders of modest means get down on their knees.

Motorcycles embody a unique dichotomy: they're material assets capable of opening spiritual pathways. Watching a big screen TV, even in your gigantic RV, cannot provide a similar experience. I wondered if the young man took in my dry bag and realized I wasn't a Four Seasons or even a Holiday Inn rider. Or did he think, just another jackass showing off his motorcycle? Was he too young to know—everything adheres to the bell curve?

After years of hard labor, one comes to understand: motorcycling may be the best use of money. It wouldn't hurt society to be more charitable. The powers that be fret over things like pronouns, indigenous rights, maga politicians, homeless shoplifting rights, and what to put on warning labels, while turning a blind eye to the welfare of those on two wheels.

Just as food banks assist those in need, in a fair and just world, there would be motorcycle banks run by NGOs for those struggling with worn sprockets. I'd donate a few litres of expensive oil now and then. Work, work, work! Getting nowhere fast, your dream bike always out of reach because you're disadvantaged. Imagine stopping by the motorcycle bank to choose a new chain, some leftover brake fluid, or one of those sheepskin seat covers?

I pulled off my helmet, willing to assist, but it doesn't work that way. Each rider must get down on their own knees and learn to flush fully. The path of motorcycle mastery isn't paved with help from salvation armies. *Young man, you must stick with your fixer, even though it might let you down or embarrass you. One day you'll reflect and know this: JOY has little to do with owning a state-of-the-art machine (unless you're dealing with a worn sprocket, needing new tires, or your turn signal is duct-taped together).*

In any case Real Riders Are Not Quitters! Never give up on yourself! I suppose that explains why there are no motorcycle bank nonprofits. We dwell on that part of the bell curve that thrives, not cries.

I logged a mental feedback note: Martin, your therapy group participants are diverse. Be on the lookout for institutional discrimination. Less fortunate, embarrassed riders on fixers may bolt. And where do they go? There are no biker shelters. All they have are groups like yours. Consider a 'No Bikes' policy for your first meeting to help newcomers feel comfortable.

A truth about motorcycles: JOY can't be bought, but possessing a decent bike raises the chances of discovering it.

Approaching the fixer, I couldn't help but picture it as a floatie neglected in a toilet bowl, needing to be fully flushed.

The young man remained focused on the bike's chain. It's the same at food banks, I suppose. Management learned long ago to separate the needy from the donor class. It avoids scenarios like, 'thanks so much for leaving those cheap instant noodles. Enjoy your steak and lobster tonight, lard ass.' To avert class conflict, fat cat food bank management teams use volunteer intermediaries, rewarding them with the joy of giving.

"Need some help?" I asked, using my Gearhead Ghandi voice.

The young man stood, looked toward Classy, and said, "Beauty."

"Yup. Unfortunately, not mine." I motioned toward the fixer. "2014... or 15?"

"Fifteen."

I nodded.

"The chain's stretched. But it'll get me home. No worries."

"Yea, they're very reliable bikes." I fibbed. "Used to own one just like it."

I could have added the sentence Smarty Marty used when I told him I'd kill to have an R69. "Don't live a slavish life wishing for a future turn of events."

I refrained from using it since the young man might have given the same response I gave Smarty: "It's easy for you to say. You already own one." Instead, I stretched my lie. "Had a ton of fun on mine." Then I offered my snack and asked, "trail mix?"

The man rubbed his greasy fingers on his jeans, poked his

hand around inside the bag, and came out with a large handful. "Thanks."

I nodded, miffed that he'd taken an inordinate number of the yogurt covered cranberries.

CHAPTER 21 - IMMUNE

Hells Angels or maybe Commandos cruised by on the opposite side of the freeway, moving away from Vancouver. Given their menacing appearance, it's easy to forget each rider began life as a law-abiding infant, grounded and compliant, their minds blank slates. We all have the freedom to decide; some choose the 'bad motherfucker' path while others become food bank volunteers. The Almighty values free will and so doesn't pin the Ten Commandments to our belly buttons. We take the human journey and it's left to each one of us to find our place.

For those choosing the outlaw club path, motorcycles are as essential as robes are to priests. You can't be a Hells Angel and drive a Prius or pedal one of those adult trikes to the clubhouse.

"It's why I don't belong to a club." Actually, Marta belongs to the Moto Guzzi Owners Club. She's the only member in our area. "Pride of ownership is fine, but be vigilant. Don't become a stereotype."

Why don't motorcycles change badasses, Martin? Move them closer to their beginner's minds. Should you be weeding them out of your community? Like how society puts outlaws in jail to separate good from bad?

Among the freeway riders, two bikes were dramatically

chopped, sporting long raked front forks that mocked the wheel's practical function. Choppers distribute little weight on the front wheel. By adding ape-hangers and positioning legs forward, the body's ability to leverage the front suspension is lost. On the two choppers, the front tires traveled in a world of their own, lonely, afraid, unable to perform as they were designed to, and always adding risk. Chopper riders have no interest in scraping pegs. Without the capacity to get body weight on top of the front brake, tire and suspension, the capability to escape or evade in emergency situations is lost. These bikes are built for show, not for agility, but still, there is wind and freedom.

I guess it's like penicillin, Martin? Some people are allergic. The Motorcycle Prescription doesn't work for everyone the same way.

◆ ◆ ◆

Witnessing a massive group of Angels commanding a road leaves an indelible impression. It's a spectacle of pure showbiz.

A couple of years before my accident, I was at a small-town gas station when thirty gang members pulled in. Their presence inspired both awe and panic. The teenage gas clerk, overwhelmed, immediately signaled defeat. Words were unnecessary; the sheer weight of the Angels' presence sufficed to assert dominance. Customers deferred, resigning themselves to wait until the exhaust smoke settled. Their unspoken plan —fade into the background so we won't provoke these bad motherfuckers.

I was chatting with a Dreamer by the pumps when we heard the roar of the gang's engines. "Holy mother of Jesus," the Dreamer swore before fleeing for the safety of his pickup truck. The bikers revved their engines and turned off the highway. They were at liberty to do whatever they chose to do. You don't poke a bear and sometimes you don't insist on full flushes.

As a precaution against saying something silly, I put my helmet on. Marta wouldn't have hesitated. "We're all riders here. Let's chat them up."

Three Angels gave me the once over. With my visor open, I flashed a weak smile, hoping not to come across as a weenie or a jackass. I was a mere nobody, so I nudged my conspicuous machine away from the pumps, keen to leave ahead of the mass exodus.

A truth about motorcycles: do not attempt to pass a large group of bad asses.

As I set off, my thoughts wandered to riders I'd met who looked like killers but turned out to be teddy bears. One confided, "If it was only about riding, I'd make some changes." His point being that he loved the camaraderie and belonging—the same reason people wear team jackets. Solo riders are a community, but it's not the same—no crests or clubhouses.

The freeway traffic lurched, its rhythm fast and then slow. Staying focused on clogged expressways can be challenging. My level of situational awareness teetered on the brink of sheer boredom. *Martin, do you think the bell curve, the 80:20 rule applies? Is it really feasible to stay completely in the moment all the time?*

A sea of lumbering trucks bogged the traffic down. Classy dipsy-doodled through the congestion before settling into the line. A half hour later, I exited and pulled into a fast-food joint for a pit stop and to contemplate heading to one of the last campgrounds before the city.

After appreciating the disinfected institutional washroom vibe, with my coffee on the table, I thumbed through the journal, hoping for insight. To camp or not to camp?

Remove Your Freeway Blinders

Awareness involves being alert to both the external environment and your internal experiences. On freeways, you may notice trucks, litter, sprawl, traffic jams, foul air, but there is more. Our thoughts shape our view of reality. Truly look and observe. There is more to see. Don't let it slip away unnoticed.

Life is life. It can never be bad. Even in the midst of the mundane, it's a miracle to exist. It can be wonderful to feel bored or uncomfortable, and it's equally wonderful not to feel bored. Everything has its magic. Let go of your preconceptions. Ride and be aware of everything around you. What's happening each second? That moment will never come again. Life is not somewhere else. Don't dismiss it. At this moment, nothing else exists.

On the freeway, as in other parts of our lives, we often find what we expect to see. Remove the blinders that confine you to the familiar.

Balance

Accountants balance books to ensure expenses are matched by income. It's the lifeblood of business. Likewise, riding can become imbalanced by excessive speed, carelessness, vanity, or disinterest. You're moving and getting somewhere, but at what cost? Allow your motorcycle to remind you—life is about equilibrium.

Instinctively, I steered Classy away from the last potential campground. We lacked for nothing; there was no deficiency that a night in a tent could make up for. I felt I was already in balance.

PART 3: HOME

CHAPTER 22 - THE
KING RETURNS

R iding through the neighborhood felt like a victory lap —Gearhead Gandhi returns! Or was it the beginning of a switch from freedom rider to trim painter? In a race, you pour everything into crossing the finish line, but ending a motorcycle road trip is bittersweet. A twinge of sadness seeped in as I anticipated bidding farewell to Classy. I longed to carve out a few more days together. Yet I felt the call of everyday routines, familiarity, friends, and family.

I logged my final feedback note. Martin, talk to your community about transitioning. Members must appreciate that ending one ride opens the door to the next.

That's when I spotted Strawberry Angelo walking her rat dog on her customary route. She hadn't heeded my advice—now it starts! Turn and walk on a different sidewalk. I felt privileged to have been a motorcycle explorer, if only for a few days.

As I switched off, Pearly's enthusiastic welcome underscored the joy of returning. Her barks, brimming with canine enthusiasm, formed a jubilant hallelujah chorus, signaling that the second greatest thing in her life was home—I was on the pillion just behind mealtime. We both love bikes, but for different reasons.

Bunny approached in his typical feline manner—nonchalant

but ever watchful. A feast of treats awaited them both, accompanied by a flurry of affectionate pats.

Dori smiled but did not brush against my leg. Better yet, she surprised me with two underbakes.

Homecomings unfold as grand celebrations, marking the end of brief nomadic lives. Gone were the worries about pitching tents, dealing with unhygienic toilets, sighting condescending signage, and fighting off snakes.

Show me the paint, I thought. And perhaps I'd suggest to Dori we volunteer at the local food bank. It was something we could do together since we no longer rode two-up. I don't think Dori would be surprised given she pictured me holding a sign, **Gearhead Ghandi**.

'Absolutely not! Dr. Peggy cannot join us,' I'd insist, or maybe paint it on a sign. **No Pissy!**

CHAPTER 23 -
SO LONG

There was time to read the last entry before going to Tony's bistro. So, with Bunny settled on my lap, I scrolled to the final thoughts in the POWER Journal.

Our True Self

Riding ushers us into a deeper reality, toward our true state where illusions are dismissed. Our lives, vibrant paintings, blur as we move. They become a kaleidoscope of shifting moments and situations. The rhythmic melody of wheels turning harmonizes with the world around us, each rotation adding a beat to our composition. Inhale deeply. Relish the sense of freedom. Let the gentle wind remind us to remain present, here and now.

We allow ourselves to be immersed in every event. We know who we are and what our purpose is. There is no confusion or conflict as we broaden our understanding. On a motorcycle, we can embrace our true selves.

We don't need miracles; we let the wind unveil the vastness of our possibilities and the unity we share with the universe.

Embrace each moment—you are the integral part of the ever-changing landscape that is your life. Ride on, my friends—let the power of motorcycles to do good, provide you with what you need.

As the screen went dark, I felt a drop of gratitude forming an overwhelming sense of wonder. Just as I was about to break down, Bunny stuck his claws into my leg as if to say, 'just pet me.'

I hugged my friend, wiped a drop of gratitude from my eye, then gave myself a kick in the ass.

Whatever Bunny. Even bikers have their true sensitive self.

At Tony's, Martin greeted me with, "You look so relaxed. Camping, I expect... an extra dose?"

"A few more twists in the road, logged, huh?" Conrad said, changing the subject. He knew the facts of the matter.

"Didn't bother unpacking," I said. "May go out again."

"The Rockies," Cam asked?

"Washroom," I said, excusing myself.

SQUIB Dolores, her eyes alight with curiosity, called after me, "Can't wait to hear about your trip, Michael. Especially the camping."

I was prepared to come clean, but when I returned, Marta stepped forward, taking control. Following a few words, Tony presented me with a slightly under-baked cinnamon roll before Marta held up my new tee-shirt. It said: **'Top Tier.'**

It wasn't a good time to time for a confession.

I walked out of Tony's with Cam. As we got close to the bikes, I expected to hear his signature yell: "Participate or die!" Instead, he said softly, "Always On."

"What? You said something, Cam?"

Cam grinned shyly.

Welcome to team Enjoy Riding More, buddy. Marta told me she also had a **Top Teir** tee shirt for Cam. "Maybe after his Rocky Mountain trip."

After waving goodbye to those heading to Benson, Marta, Smarty Marty, Tony and I went inside. Tony had bistro business to attend to. The three of us sat to say so long. Marty would leave for San Josc the following day.

"I've fallen in love with Classy," I confessed, hoping to summon my 'I do what I want to do' spirit and demand Smarty sell me his R69S. "It's become more than a machine... we're kindred spirits. Therapeutic," I added. "And I'd be a roving ambassador for your work. What'd think?"

Marty responded with a nod, providing a glimmer of hope. "I'll keep my eyes peeled for another one. It's possible... I could pass Bitty on to you and do another rebuild."

Delighted, I said, "I'm your buyer."

"Not that it really matters," Marta added. "You have a perfectly good bike, Mike. Remember: the wheels are round and they roll? If you understand that, you don't need anything else."

Whatever, Marta. Ever try riding an understanding?

"Classics just roll better, Marta." Marty smiled.

Truly a wise man.

Marta replied with one word. "Guzzi."

A little while later, I left; it's not a good idea to stretch 'so longs' out. "Got trim to paint," I said, as if it were mandatory, like when you're running on empty and must fill your tank.

Before beginning my chore, I painted this on the garage wall above 'Motorcycle on Velvet:'

Now It Starts!

The methodical action of my paint strokes matched the rhythm in my mind. I could hear the sound of wheels on asphalt. *Painting the trim clears the way for the motorcycle prescription.* But I didn't think of it as a goal.

THANKS!

Thanks Reader! If you enjoyed the book, please consider leaving a review, just a few words will help others discover *The Motorcycle Prescription* and will be greatly appreciated.

Say hello. Questions? Comments?
Contact the author: messenger - Scraping Pegs on Facebook or beatenstickpress@gmail.com.

BOOKS BY THIS AUTHOR

Scraping Pegs, The Truth About Motorcycles

Ten Motorcycle Riding Rules and the author meets Horace the Horrible.

The Joy Of Motorcycles, More Scraping Pegs

An enquiry into joy and recovering from Horace the Horrible.

Scrape Your Lists, The Motorcycle Files

The motorcycle experience expressed in point form.

Motorcycle State Of Mind, Beyond Scraping Pegs

Why ride a motorcycle? Every revolution of the wheel is an opportunity when you read between the lines.

Printed in Great Britain
by Amazon

0fde4e46-96cb-4e83-bc68-8f95d47b908eR01